Do You See This Woman?

Clearer Vision Through Jesus' Eyes

Valerie Baker

PRESS

Do You See This Woman?
by Valerie Baker

Printed in the United States of America

ISBN 978-1-60034-925-6

www.xulonpress.com

To all my sisters in South Africa, whose warm welcome, gracious hospitality and loving encouragement inspired and motivated me to move from dreaming to doing so that this book would become a reality

And to my family, for their patience, support, understanding and encouragement when I was in "author mode"

I lovingly dedicate this book

Table of Contents

Acknowledgements

First of all, thank you to my husband, Larry, who has supported me, believed in me, and cheered me on as I wrote this. I also want to thank Allen Whitacre and Karen Close for reading the manuscript and sharing their comments with me.

I am grateful to the many people who have taught me through the years. It would be impossible to name them without leaving someone out who was important in my spiritual training. I received a strong Biblical foundation from the men and women who taught the Sunday morning and Wednesday evening Bible classes in the church where I grew up. I can still remember the sound of their voices and the lessons I learned from them, even though some have long since gone on to their reward. The men whose preaching I have been privileged to hear in the churches I have attended and those who taught and preached at youth camps and rallies I attended in my teens had a priceless impact on my life.

The Bible professors at Michigan Christian College (now known as Rochester College, but always MCC to me) built on that foundation at a time when my walk of faith was somewhat precarious. I may have seemed sleepy in your classes, but I did enjoy them and received many benefits from what you taught. I have also benefited greatly from Bible teaching on the radio as I went about my tasks as a homemaker through the years.

I am especially grateful to Jeff Walling, whose sermon on "Simonosis" planted the seed in my mind for this book, almost eighteen years ago. Jerry Jones is one of my heroes, for making God's grace and power to change my life real to me, and for encouraging my husband and me to pursue our dreams and advising us how to get started.

So many people have made a difference in my life, I am amazed when I remember how many individuals contributed to my knowledge and understanding of God's word. For that reason, it is impossible for me to remember where many of my ideas have originated. If anyone reading this recognizes an idea they taught me, I hope they will understand. God knows who you are, and He will richly reward you. As for me, I am forever in your debt.

I would like to thank my friend Aimee Ping, who gave me my first opportunity to share these concepts at a ladies' retreat. It was fun, encouraging, and very special. Let's do another one sometime.

Preface

We can find it far too easy to read Scripture on a surface level without recognizing the personhood of the people on its pages. We read about the widow whose son died without any thought about what that was like for her. Then we read that Jesus comes along , raises her son to life and gives him back to her, and move on to the next verse as if that were a common, everyday occurrence. Was that how she or Jesus saw it? Did she have no feelings about what had just happened? Have you ever given a thought to the impact Jesus had on her life? Or even how Jesus felt when He gave her such a gift?

I have attempted to enter into the minds and hearts of the people with whom Jesus interacted in hopes that they would come alive for us as real people. It is my hope that as we see them more clearly, through Jesus' eyes, we'll be better able to understand what a difference He can make in lives touched by Him. My prayer is that we will see what a wonderful Savior He is, and adopt His vision in the way we see ourselves, our family and friends, the people we know, and those we tend to overlook, ignore or even reject. How did Jesus treat the unlovable, the untouchable, the hopeless, or the socially unacceptable? What does He want us to learn from Him? I have been so bold as to attempt to enter into His mind and heart as He met these people. My thoughts are based on what I understand about His nature and character and what He taught. I hope I have not misrepresented Him in any way.

I went into great detail about how the woman caught in adultery ended up there. I realize this is not necessarily how it happened, but it is how I've seen it happen in the lives of people I know personally. I wrote it this way in hopes that it will help us to have more compassion on those who have fallen and to guard ourselves against falling in the same way. If we do not guard ourselves, it can happen whether we think it can or not. There is not always a predatory individual and a victim as I portrayed it here, although there can be. More often, two people are caught off guard in vulnerable circumstances and find themselves in a situation they never intended. I portrayed it the way I did because it seems to me that one of the Pharisees trapped this woman by seducing her, just to attempt to trap Jesus by using her. Otherwise, where was her "partner in crime" and why was he not dragged out to be stoned along with her?

At any rate, my hope is that you will take a closer look at the people in Scripture, dig deeper for the lessons to be learned, and come away with a richer, fuller understanding and love for God and for people.

Introduction

A lone woman plods along the desert road, her shoulders bent as if toiling under a heavy burden. Her mind relentlessly searches for solutions to her dilemma. Having recently become pregnant, the ramifications made her home life unbearable, so she is running away. Her problems hound her—nowhere to go, no source of income, no one to care for her. In addition, her parched throat reminds her that she has had no water to drink for far too long. Suddenly her eyes light up as she spots a spring up ahead. "Oh, please let it be real and not a mirage!" she cries out, thinking that no one hears her. But then she jumps out of her skin as a voice speaks her name,

"Hagar, servant of Sarai, where have you come from, and where are you going?"

"I'm running away from my mistress Sarai," she answered.

Then the angel of the Lord told her, "Go back to your mistress and submit to her."

The angel added, "I will so increase your descendants that they will be too numerous to count."

The angel of the Lord also said to her:

"You are now with child
  and you will have a son.
You shall name him Ishmael,
  for the Lord has heard of your misery.
He will be a wild donkey of a man;
  his hand will be against everyone
    and everyone's hand against him,
  and he will live in hostility
    toward all his brothers."

She gave this name to the Lord who spoke to her: "You are the God who sees me," for she said, "I have now seen the One who sees me." That is why the well was called Beer Lahai Roi; it is still there, between Kadesh and Bered. (Gen. 16:8-14)

He is the God who *sees* me. Wow. Do you ever get so wrapped up in your problems, you see no solutions, you lie awake at night, your stomach stays tied up in knots, and you think that no one sees you? Can you find rest in the assurance that you are not alone, that your cries are heard, and that you are not invisible or unloved? Can you see what purpose and meaning your life could have if you looked for people who struggle this way and told them about the One who sees them, hears their cries, and loves them intensely?

Jesus said, "Anyone who has seen me has seen the Father." (John 14:9) He demonstrated time and time again that our Father is "the God who sees me." Let's journey together through the pages of Scripture and learn from Jesus more about this wonderful God.

CHAPTER 1

Recognized by Reputation

Simon tried unsuccessfully to hide his disgust. He found the scene before him utterly unbelievable. This man who was supposedly a prophet sat there and allowed this vile creature to throw herself all over Him. She drenched His feet with her tears and used her hair as a towel to wipe them. Not only that, but she actually kissed His feet and poured perfume on them. Not just any perfume, but very expensive perfume. He could only imagine how she had "earned" enough money to buy that perfume. He wondered where his servants were when she came to the door and why they had allowed her to enter his house. She certainly wasn't invited. He was definitely beginning to regret that he had invited this so-called prophet to have dinner with him. This was not what he had in mind when he invited Him, that's for sure. How could the man possibly not recognize just by looking at her what kind of woman she was? Everyone else in the room did; it was obvious they felt very uncomfortable with the scene before them. If He did see her for who she was, how could He let her even come near Him, let alone touch Him and kiss His feet? What a fake He turned out to be. Oh well, that's pretty much what he had expected anyway.

The woman was known only by her reputation. Everyone in the world seemed to know about her and the things she had done. She knew not to expect anything but disdain and abuse from anyone. Everyone she had ever known either used her or ignored her. Religious people communicated with their eyes, and sometimes with their words, nothing but ridicule and condemnation. No way would she ever want to go near a synagogue or the temple or anywhere else that those people frequented. Why go there when she knew it meant subjecting herself to more guilt and shame than she already carried with her everywhere she went? But she had heard about a rabbi who was different. He traveled all over Judea teaching and healing people. Even better than that as far as she was concerned, He treated people like her completely differently. He went so far as to seek them out, and seemed to enjoy their company. She found it hard to believe, but she had been assured that it was true. She just had to see for herself. Would He turn out to be just like everyone else, and make her feel lower than dirt?

When she finally encountered Him, her wildest imaginings could not have prepared her for the experience. She feared to even look at Him, but He reached out and lifted her chin so that she had to look into His eyes. What she saw there she never would have dreamed possible. His eyes radiated a love that in all her life she had never experienced. Although she searched intently, she did not find an ounce of condemnation. Those eyes spoke only of compassion, mercy, acceptance, and hope. She knew that He had to know about her lifestyle by the way she dressed and the gossiping tongues that showed her no mercy. And yet He treated her so kindly and lovingly. She had no memory of anyone who had ever looked at her with love like that. She knew with all her heart that her life changed forever in that moment when she looked into those eyes. She wanted to sing and dance and shout for joy! She was about to tell Him how much His love and kindness meant to her when someone in His entourage reminded Him that He had a dinner engagement and it was time to go.

She decided that she had to see Him again, so she followed behind to see where they were going. Then she quickly ran home to get the most valuable thing she owned. She needed it to help her express her love and gratitude to Him for showing her the only compassion she had ever known. Besides, her purpose for splurging on that extravagant perfume had changed in an instant.

As she drew nearer to the house He had entered, she fought down the anxiety beginning to grip her heart. With every step she took, its intensity increased. But she summoned her courage, reminded herself of her purpose, and willed herself to keep going. Oh, why did He have to be having dinner in *that* house?

She knew exactly what kind of treatment to expect from their household. They would certainly refuse her entrance if they saw her coming. She was relieved to see some stragglers walking in, and blended herself in with them. No one noticed her, just as she had hoped.

The minute she laid eyes on Him again, her heart burst with adoration for Him. Even if she wanted to, she couldn't keep from doing what her heart demanded of her. In that instant she no longer cared what anyone else thought about her, but only about worshipping this wonderful person before her. Tears filled her eyes, spilled over her cheeks and poured onto His dusty feet. Her tears began to turn the dust on them into a muddy stream, so she impulsively loosened her thick hair and used it to wipe them clean. She couldn't help but kiss them, they were so beautiful to her. Then she opened the perfume, and as she poured it over His feet, her heart overflowed with praise and thanksgiving. She was amazed that He was willing to receive the adoration of someone like her. Her eyes caught a glimpse of the Pharisee staring at her, but she refused to be troubled at all by the disgust on his face. She knew she was in the presence of One who placed real value on her, no matter what she had done, and she cared only about what His eyes told her.

He interrupted her thoughts when He began to speak directly to Simon. He told him a story about money lending and debts and inability to pay, and she wondered how it related to the present situation. Then he turned toward her and looked into her face again with those wonderful loving eyes. When He continued speaking, she realized He was still talking to Simon rather than to her. He asked Simon if he saw "this woman" and then, to her amazement, He listed the Pharisee's offenses against Him, and praised her actions toward Him. The man who was so judgmental of her, and took pride in his own righteousness, had neglected the rules of common courtesy toward his guest. He had demonstrated by his rudeness that he didn't care much about Him. She, on the other hand, loved Him completely because she believed He had forgiven her of so much. Just in case she had any seeds of doubt, although He acknowledged that her sins were many, He also declared them forgiven in the hearing of this whole crowd of "good people". He told her that her faith had saved her, and to go in peace. Go in peace she would certainly do; this had been the best day of her entire life.

The woman was starving to death for love and compassion, and He wasn't about to send her away empty-hearted. Even though she was searching, she couldn't bring herself to look up at Him. Therefore, He lifted her face so that she couldn't help but look into His, and spoke with His eyes of His love, mercy and grace. The light in her eyes and the joy on her face reflected her understanding of His message. He also wanted her to hear the words from His lips that He had forgiven her sins, but it would have to wait. He intended for other ears to hear that conversation, and they were yet to be assembled. The time had come, though, when they were beginning to come together; it was time to go and join them.

He knew she would follow them because it was obvious she wanted to speak to Him. She wouldn't rest until she had the opportunity. She had no way of knowing, but He planned for her to assist Him that evening in His effort to open blind eyes and teach important truths. When they arrived at the home of their dinner host, Simon, He noted that she quickly departed in the direction of her home. She would soon return, He knew, and together they would deliver the message of the evening. For now, He and His companions entered the house and reclined at the table. As other guests continued to arrive, the delicious aromas of the coming meal whetted their appetites. He planned to provide nourishment of a different kind, and His preparations were almost complete. As soon as she arrived, He could begin to serve it up. Meanwhile, He searched the faces of the other guests, and prayed that their eyes and hearts would open up to His message.

Soon she appeared, and without realizing it, commenced with the lesson of the evening. She was completely enthralled with Him, and her adoration and gratitude welled up in her heart and spilled from her eyes in the form of tears. With total abandon, she expressed her devotion to Him, and He was delighted with her. She provided a perfect picture of humility as she washed and dried His feet and poured her perfume on them. That kind of humility pleased Him, given that it moves a soul to kneel before Him to ask for and receive forgiveness of sins. He only granted it to those who humbled themselves and asked.

However, as the scent of her perfume drifted through the air, Simon's countenance filled with disgust. Jesus heard his thoughts as clearly as if he had spoken them aloud. Oh Simon, if you would just open your heart and look with fresh eyes, you would see that I am indeed a Prophet and so much more. You are in the presence of your High Priest and your King, but because He's not the king you've been expecting, you fail to see Him when He's right here in front of you. He didn't come to free you from the grip of Rome, but rather from the grip of your sin. He came to lift your heavy burden of trying to keep every tiny detail of the Law, with the added weight of the interpretations and traditions piled onto it by you and your Pharisee brothers. He came to set you free, Simon, to soar as if on eagles' wings in the freedom of living in relationship with the Father. Your obedience is important, yes, but the motivation for it is just as important. Love will inspire you to do for the Father what rules and regulations can never do. You could see this clearly, if you would observe the demonstration of it by this woman who has discovered such freedom this very day.

Yes, He knew who was touching Him and exactly what kind of woman she was. She was a precious lamb who was lost, and her Shepherd left everything to find her. Had Simon ever once wondered what she had experienced in her life that could have led her into captivity to the evil one, who oppressed her for so long? Did it ever occur to him that she might have had her innocence stolen from her, rather than surrendered by her? If she had concluded she was worthless and didn't deserve anything better, what had he done but reinforce that conclusion? True, she was a sinner, but Simon was one as well, and Jesus loved both of them enough to die for them. There was so much more to her than her sins, but Simon and many others had pronounced judgment on her and ostracized her without ever seeing who she really was.

Simon needed a word picture to clarify his vision. Two debtors, one with a small debt and one with a substantial one, were *both* unable to pay their debts. That was an important point that he must not miss. If the lender cancelled the debts of both, who would love him more? Of course, the one with the bigger debt cancelled. Simon may have owed a smaller debt than this woman did, but was just as unable to pay and stood in need of forgiveness as much as she did. Forgiveness was available to him, but he perceived little need to ask for it and therefore received little of it. Thus, he had little love for the Lord from whom he needed it.

His focus on keeping rules produced the fruits of self-righteousness, hypocrisy, arrogance and a critical spirit toward those he perceived as rule-breakers. Because he placed his confidence in himself, fear prevented him from honestly facing his shortcomings, because to do so would undermine that confidence. Therefore, he had to push any self-doubt to the back of his mind and keep it imprisoned there behind a wall of hardheartedness, and keep telling himself how righteous he was.

Jesus knew that Simon needed His grace and mercy, but Simon couldn't see it. And He wanted to give him what he needed. With the precision and skill of a surgeon with his scalpel, He cut right through to the heart of Simon's problem with the telling of the story. By shifting his attention to generic debtors and lender, He darted right past the defensive wall to capture his interest. Since Simon was blind to his own indebtedness, Jesus listed one by one the ways he had discourteously treated the Guest he had invited into his home. It was obvious that his motive for inviting Him had not been love or even simple friendship. The most basic expectations of common courtesy dictated that a host provide water for the washing of feet and greet guests with a kiss. Simon's rudeness violated the simple command to love his neighbor, making him a lawbreaker. (Leviticus 19:18)

This woman, on the other hand, loved Him with her whole being, and demonstrated it without reservation. Oh children, behold her and learn from her! Everyone present knew she was guilty of many sins, as she was also painfully aware. She'd never be allowed to forget it even if she tried. She desperately needed a fresh start that only her Savior could give her. Beyond that, she needed to be given back her dignity, and be respected as a human being, created and loved by God. He knew if He didn't open the eyes of the others to see beyond all the labels they had attached to her, then they would never see the new life she was beginning. Unfortunately, He recognized the tendency of people to be blind to any changes in each other. Call it the syndrome of "Once a_____, always a_____". So He simply asked Simon to *see* her, not as a "sinner", an "outcast", an "untouchable" or whatever else, but as a woman.

Not only did He see her as a woman, a person of worth, but He also expressed His pleasure in her total devotion to Him. What He wanted from her, from Simon, and from every other person He created was for them to love Him with all of their being. As sinful as she was, she gave Him this, while so many others who thought they knew how to please God did not. Neither did they grasp who He was and why He was there among them. Their preconceived ideas of what their Messiah would look like obscured their vision when He was right there in front of them. And because they misconstrued God's expectations of His children, they couldn't accept that He would have anything to do with "those kind of people". They were appalled that He would purposely seek them out and keep company with them. They ignored what God had instructed His prophet to tell His people, "I desire mercy, not sacrifice."(Hosea 6:6)

He was aware that He completely upended their notions of what it meant to be righteous, when He scathingly rebuked those who took great pride in their own goodness, while seemingly condoning the actions of those who they judged wicked. They failed to see that He never condoned sin, but just loved the sinful and offered them hope that He would help them change what they could not on their own. They needed to realize that rejection never motivates anyone to improve their lives; and comprehend how impossible it is for His children to be truly righteous with human strength. He was the only human who was without sin, the only one who had a right to throw stones at the guilty, and instead of stones, He planned to take nails in His hands for them.

If only He could open their eyes to Him, to their own need, and to the needs of one another. Realistically, He knew that He would reach some quite readily, that others would take a very long time to come around, and that no matter what He said or did to reveal Himself as the Son of God, some would choose to remain in their blind, lost state. They were the ones who completely broke His heart.

Take a closer look:
1. Read Luke 7:36-50. With whom do you most closely identify in this story?
   What changes do you need to make in the way you see Jesus? Yourself? Other people? What labels have you attached to yourself or someone else that you need to discard from your vocabulary?
2. Read Matthew 9:10-13. What answer did Jesus give the Pharisees when they questioned Him about His choice of dining companions?
3. Read Mark 12:28-34, Romans 7:21-8:4 and James 2:8-13. What commandments are most important to God? By what law do you want to be judged?
4. Have you ever allowed yourself to worship the Lord with such complete abandon that you didn't care what anyone else thought about it? What might happen if you did? If you ever witnessed someone worshipping

Him in that way, what kind of response might they receive from you? What has Jesus taught you about God's perspective on it?

5. When a "sinner" visits your congregation or spends time with you, will they "go in peace" as if they've been in Jesus' presence, or will they be turned off to Christianity by your attitude towards them?

CHAPTER 2

Desperate Daughters

So many years had passed since she had been well that she barely remembered how it felt. If she had any idea when she first became ill that she would still be in this condition twelve years later, she might have long since willed herself to die. As it was, she had used up all her resources and felt worse than ever.

She had reached the point of desperation when she heard about a man named Jesus who traveled around preaching about the kingdom of God and healing the sick. If only He would come near enough for her to meet Him without a crowd of people surrounding Him. Because of her bleeding, if anyone touched her, it rendered them unclean according to the Law. Anyone who knew about her situation would be sure to drive her away if she tried to come anywhere near Him. She resigned herself once again to her plight and wondered rather hopelessly what she would do next.

All at once, she heard a commotion outside. It sounded like the entire population of the town was right outside her door. She overheard a man whose voice strained with severe pain saying he just had to reach Jesus before it was too late. Apparently, his daughter was on her deathbed, and he hoped Jesus would come and heal her. That meant Jesus was right there in her hometown! Suddenly she forgot all about laws, uncleanness, and crowds, and her only thought was to get out there and follow those men until they led her to Him.

As she fought her way through the crowd, her previous thoughts returned, and fear with them, but she was not about to stop now. She determined that she would hide her face with her shawl and try not to draw attention to herself. From what she had heard about Jesus, she felt sure she could just touch His cloak and she would be healed. Her excitement at the prospect infused her weakened body with the strength to keep going until she reached her goal. She only had to get close enough to reach in and touch the edge of His cloak, and then she could blend back into the crowd. Blending in certainly should not be difficult, since the crowd was jammed so close together they were practically crushing Him.

As she came nearer, she recognized one of the men she had followed as Jairus, the synagogue ruler, on his knees before Jesus pleading for him to help his daughter. Good, that was just the distraction she needed to quickly and quietly accomplish her mission and she could be back home before anyone took notice of her. She would have to prove she was well before she would be accepted in public. Besides, she didn't want to divert Jesus' attention when Jairus so desperately needed Him to tend to his daughter.

She forced her way in close enough to squeeze her hand through, and as soon as she sensed the cloth on her fingertips, she felt more alive than she ever had before! Oh what a feeling! She knew the bleeding had stopped, and noticed the color returning to her skin.

As she rejoiced in her newfound health, she suddenly became aware that He was persistently asking who touched Him. His followers seemed to think the question foolish, with so many people pressing around Him, but He said He had felt power go out from Him. She realized that it was too late to quietly sneak away unnoticed, so she fearfully stepped forward and told Him the whole story, right there in front of everyone. Not really knowing what to expect, warmth and peace filled her when He called her His daughter and told her that her faith had healed her. She could go in peace, freed from her suffering.

Before it occurred to her that she must thank Him, some men came up and told Jairus that it was too late; his daughter was dead. The woman felt sorry that she had distracted Jesus, but then He told Jairus not to be afraid but believe, and the girl would be healed. She couldn't speak for Jairus, but she had no doubt that everything was about to be set right for him just like it had been for her.

Jesus had seen crowds before, but this one was especially pushy. Everyone tried to get next to Him at once, making it difficult for anyone but those closest in to have any chance at success. The ones who would succeed would be the ones so desperate for Him that they'd let nothing stop them. He could tell exactly which members of this particular crowd fit that description. He knew what they sought from Him, and He anticipated their joy when He gave it to them with immense pleasure. He was pleased as well because so many of His children would have the opportunity that day to see God's glory and grow in faith.

The first one to reach Him was Jairus. His anguish over his daughter was quite evident, and Jesus was happy to know that He was able to ease it. But before He could respond to Jairus' pleading, He felt His healing power flow out from within Him. It meant that His other desperate seeker had arrived. He was well aware that she hoped to escape the scrutiny of the crowd, and that Jairus would become even more agitated by any delay. Nevertheless, He intended to take time to focus the attention of the crowd upon her, for their benefit as well as hers.

Before her neighbors would restore her to her place in the community, they needed to witness that she was whole and clean. Their perception of her as the sickly, unclean and needy person she had been for so many years must be put to rest. And so He asked who touched Him, and kept asking until she came forward and knelt before Him. To His great satisfaction, she testified of her healing without any prompting. She explained how she believed that if she just touched the edge of His cloak she'd be healed. At the very instant she succeeded in doing so, it happened exactly as she expected. Her great faith merged with His great power and compassion to restore her health. Her faith delighted Him, and He wanted them all to know it. So He said to her, "Daughter, your faith has healed you."(Mark 5:34) By calling her "Daughter" He demonstrated to the townspeople her worth to Him. Then He sent her away in peace, lighthearted and free. He had to get going; He had another precious daughter to restore to her health.

Take a closer look:
1. Read Matthew 9:20-22, Mark 5:25-34, and Luke 8:43-48 and note the subtle differences in each account. What do those details reveal to you?
2. Read Leviticus 15:25-27 to learn about the regulations regarding uncleanness.
3. Do you suppose when this woman first fell ill, people helped her and tended to her needs? After twelve years, how many might still be around to care for her? Today, do you know anyone who will faithfully care for a chronically ill person for a long period of time, without becoming impatient with them? What might you learn from them? Do you know anyone who might need your help in this way? How could you share the responsibilities with other Christian sisters?
4. Do you *see* the victims of AIDS and other scary diseases, and seek ways of ministering to their needs, or ignore them and hope they

go away? What does Jesus call you to do for them? What (or whom) do they need the most? What do their loved ones need from you?

CHAPTER 3

Widow's Wealth

She patiently waited for an opportunity to add her offering to the temple treasury. The place was packed with people, and many of them appeared to be deliberately taking their time. They casually tossed in their coins as if they hadn't a care in the world. If the coins were numerous, they made a delightful noise when they threw them in. Then heads turned to see who had made such a large contribution, which she suspected was the desired effect. She knew no one would ever have such an occasion to look her way, and she'd be embarrassed if they did. Her two little coins couldn't make enough noise to be audible to the people standing right next to her. She wouldn't want them to notice how small her offering was anyway. It wasn't much, but it was all she had, and she was glad she had it to give.

Rich folks often looked down on her because she was so poor, but she was at a loss to know what she could possibly do about it. It wasn't her fault her husband died and left her with no means of support, nor was it his. He certainly hadn't died so soon intentionally. Unfortunately, it just turned out that way.

She perceived the belief among the wealthy that poverty was a result of God's judgment for some kind of wickedness in one's life. Conversely, they thought God blessed them with wealth to reward their goodness. Well, she knew she had tried her best to live righteously, and she rested every night with her conscience clear. She was also acquainted with some of those wealthy people throwing their money around, and knew they were capable of some rotten behavior, especially in the way they treated vulnerable people like her. Because of it, she didn't accept those notions at all.

She trusted in God's goodness, and believed He'd take care of His children as any good Father would, whether they behaved or not. He blessed those who loved Him in a myriad of ways, and worldly wealth was least among them. He had richly blessed her in spite of the poverty and hardships she experienced, and she depended on Him completely. Often she found herself wondering what she'd do when her current supplies ran out, but she refused to worry; God had always provided for her. She knew that He always would because He had faithfully supplied whatever she truly needed throughout her life.

Jesus intently observed the crowds as they put their money into the temple treasury. He had a seat with a clear view of everything going on there. He had just been teaching in the temple, where a large crowd listened to Him with delight. He warned them to beware of those who played at religion, enjoyed the attention and prestige it brought to them, and prayed lengthy prayers just to show off. They were teachers of the law who completely failed to see the point of the law they taught. If they understood it and honestly cared about obeying it, they would look after widows and provide for them, not devour their houses. Their religion, which so impressed the naive, did not impress Him at all. The tinkling noise of their pretentious offerings failed to impress Him as well. He knew they'd never miss what they so casually tossed in there. He clearly perceived their true motivation for giving, how empty it was.

Then He detected something that really did impress Him, or rather someone. He glanced around to see if any of His followers noticed her, but they were caught up in the false generosity on display. He wanted to help them see all this from His point of view, so He gathered them around and called their attention to the one who had so impressed Him. They were dumbfounded when He said she gave more than all the others. They thought He could not be serious. She obviously had to be the poorest person in sight, so how could she possibly give more than those wearing such fine clothes and tossing so many coins into the treasury? Jesus insisted that she really had.

He knew they never would have noticed her if He had not pointed her out to them.

Since He looked past external appearances into the hearts of the givers, He confidently assured them that she gave her all. Compared to what the others kept back, their offerings barely amounted to anything. Possessing so much wealth, they found it very difficult to comprehend their need for God. They were deceived into thinking they could live just fine on their own, with very little help from Him. They suffered from true poverty, the poverty of the spirit. She demonstrated by giving everything she had, as little as it was, that she placed her life wholly in God's hands and counted on Him to provide whatever she needed. She possessed authentic wealth, since she belonged to the One who in reality owned everything. There was nothing she needed that He could not give her. Because she trusted Him, she was fully committed to Him, and He was delighted to call her His child.

Take a closer look:
1. Read Mark 12:37b-44. What is the significance of this event in the context of Jesus' warnings about the teachers of the law?
2. Read 2 Corinthians 8:1-5 & 12. What similarities do you see between the widow and the Macedonian churches?
3. Read Malachi 3:8-12. Have you ever tested God in this way? If so, what was your experience?
4. Read Matthew 6:1-4 & 19-34. Which of these teachings of Jesus convict your heart? What will you do about them?

5. Read 1Timothy 6: 6-10 & 17-19. What perspectives on wealth do you gain from these instructions?

6. Do you *see* the poor around you? Have you considered how you could help them? What do they have to offer that would enable them to participate in improving their lives while preserving their dignity? What can you do to bring them to dependence on God rather than on you?

7. Which is easier, to give money or to build relationship? Which is more effective in lifting up the less fortunate to a higher standard of living?

CHAPTER 4

Persistence Pays

As her little girl's anguished screams pierced the air like a knife, she thought she would surely go mad. The child's distress and her powerlessness to do anything to ease it tortured her. With every fiber of her being, she despised the demon that relentlessly attacked her beloved daughter. She cried out to God continually, but it seemed like her prayers fell on deaf ears. Day after day, the agony continued. Is God even real, she wondered, and if He is, why doesn't He help her? She's just a child—why does He let her suffer like this? As she wrestled with these disquieting questions, her weariness from the sleepless nights and the constant turmoil threatened to overwhelm her.

A knock at her door interrupted her troubled thoughts. She glanced out the window and saw that her neighbor stood there. He often stopped by, not for neighborly visits, but to express his irritation about the dreadful racket emanating from her house. Expecting another verbal assault from him, she reluctantly opened the door. To her surprise, he appeared hopeful rather than irate. He said he'd heard about a Jewish rabbi who apparently had the power to drive out demons and heal the sick. He said he had seen a group of men early that morning, before dawn, quietly walk into town and enter a house nearby. He had the impression they wanted to keep their presence a secret. He thought it might be the rabbi and His followers. Perhaps He would be willing to help her little girl, if she hurried and asked Him before anyone else learned of His presence and formed a crowd around Him.

She immediately determined that she was going to find out. She was willing to try anything to free her daughter from the terrible torment she had to endure. Leaving the child in the care of a trusted servant, she made her way to the house. Concerned that He might refuse her because she was a Gentile, she cried out before she even got to the door, "Lord, Son of David, have mercy on me! My daughter is suffering terribly from demon-possession." (Matthew 15:22)

She noticed someone looking out the window, but He said not a word. So she continued to cry out for help, hoping desperately that He would take pity on her. Someone urged the rabbi to send her away because she kept crying out, moving her to plead even more frantically. Finally, the door opened and the rabbi stood before her.

To her dismay, He said His mission was only to the lost sheep of Israel, and her heart sank. She had nowhere else to turn! She fell at His feet and begged Him to drive the demon out of her little girl. He told her that the children must be allowed to eat all they want first, because it wasn't right to take the children's bread and toss it to their dogs.

Oh no, it was just as she had feared! What could she possibly say to that? Then it occurred to her that even the dogs are allowed to eat the children's crumbs that fall from their masters' table. Couldn't He spare her just a few crumbs' worth of His mighty power? Wouldn't that be enough to give her daughter relief? Surely the children would never miss it.

She stole a glance up to His face and was relieved to see a smile there and a twinkle in His eyes. Hope began to well up in her, and it sprang to life as He assured her that her request was granted. He commended her for her great faith. It may have been great then, but it was multiplied immeasurably when she ran home and saw her sweet little daughter. She was sleeping peacefully for the first time in ages, with the most serene, angelic expression on her beautiful little face. The mother's eyes overflowed with tears of profound relief and overwhelming joy, and she lifted them up to heaven with a prayer of praise and thanksgiving on her lips.

Ever since He had received the news that Herod had beheaded John the Baptist, Jesus had been trying to get away to pray and process His feelings. He hoped to give His disciples time to rest as well, and to hear more about their experiences while they were out teaching and healing. They had barely begun to brief Him before the crowds interrupted them. They traveled by boat to a more quiet place, but the crowds beat them to their destination on foot. When He saw them, He had compassion on them and healed their sick and fed their hungry spirits with teaching. By that time the people were worn out and physically hungry, so He took pity on them and miraculously multiplied a few fish and loaves of bread so that everyone could have enough to eat and be satisfied. Then He sent His weary disciples back into the boat to head for Bethsaida, telling them He'd catch up to them later.

After dismissing the crowd, He was finally able to steal away for some quiet time alone with His Father. When He was finished, He "caught up" to the disciples in the middle of the lake, where they strained against a contrary wind. He amazed and terrified them by walking to the boat on the water, but it moved them to worship Him when the winds died down after He boarded.

Upon landing, they were again recognized and followed wherever they went by people bringing their sick loved ones to Him for healing. Then He had been accosted by some Pharisees and teachers of the law about His disciples not keeping the traditions of the elders. It exasperated Him that they placed more emphasis on things they read into the law that weren't even there than what was clearly decreed, such as loving God and loving their neighbors, for example. Honor father and mother, take care of widows and orphans, do justice and love mercy, and principles such as that. As much as their distorted focus frustrated Him, it did present many opportunities for

Him to clarify the principles behind the commands to those who kept their hearts open to hear. Therefore, He spent some more time teaching and then attempted once again to get away with His disciples for a while. They departed that place and went to the area of Tyre and Sidon, and quietly entered a house there. (See Matthew 14 & 15 and Mark 6 & 7)

Before long, they heard a commotion and realized they had been discovered once again. A woman cried out to Him with a volume that clearly matched her level of distress. He knew she'd never give up until she got what she came for. She appeared to be at the end of her rope and hard pressed to endure her daughter's suffering for one more day. But what if He allowed her to demonstrate for His disciples how to persist in prayer and never give up? His parable of the persistent widow standing before the unjust judge came to mind (Luke 18:1-8). He would play the role of the judge, while the woman at His feet already played her role quite convincingly.

At first, He ignored her, and pretended He did not intend to help her. He told the disciples He had been sent only to the lost sheep of Israel (although the plan had always been to make salvation available to every nation in due time). She responded to His words by begging and pleading even more stridently for mercy. So He told her that it wouldn't be right to give to "dogs" the bread that was intended for the children. Her faith-filled response conveyed to Him, "A dog I may be, but I'm still depending on my Master to give me what I need." Her faith impressed Him, and He told her so. Then He declared her request granted.

The hope and joy that sprang to life in her eyes at that moment refreshed His spirit. As she rushed out the door to go see for herself that her daughter was released from her torment, He turned to His disciples with a smile on His face, and began to share with them the things that were on His heart.

Take a closer look:
1. Read Matthew 15:21-28 & Mark 7:24-30. Why did Jesus grant the mother's request?
2. Read and compare: Amos 9:11-12 & Acts 15:16-18; Isaiah 11:10 & Romans 15:12; Isaiah 9:1-2 & Matthew 4:15-16; Isaiah 42:6-7, 49:6 & Luke 4:28-32; Matthew 28:18-20, Acts 1:8 & Romans 1:16. Based on these passages, when Jesus said that He was sent only to the lost sheep of Israel, was He talking about timing rather than rejecting the woman because she was a Gentile?
3. For further study, see Acts 9:15; Acts 10:1-11:18; Acts 13:46-48 & 14:27; Acts 27:17-23; Romans 9:1-5, 24-26; Romans 3:29-30; Galatians 3:6-9 & 14; and Ephesians 3:6.
4. Do you believe Jesus really saw this woman as a dog? Could He have been testing her to help her grow in faith or to demonstrate her faith to His disciples? Or possibly using irony to help His disciples realize He cared for the Gentiles and not just Israel? Based on Acts 10:34-35, is there anyone of any nationality or race that Jesus doesn't care about? How about you?

5. What can you learn from this woman about praying for your children (or anyone else you care about)?

CHAPTER 5

Grief Becomes Gladness

She tried not to think too far into the future. It was challenging enough to survive the next few minutes. She appreciated the many friends and neighbors from town who encircled her and offered their moral support. But as her eyes fell once again on the coffin carrying her only son, a fresh wave of grief washed over her and threatened to drown her. Her husband had already died much too soon, and now she faced the future bereaved of her son. He was supposed to outlive her and take care of her in her old age, not leave her so long before his time. What was she to do? How could she go on? She wanted to die herself. She had shed so many tears, she wondered how she could possibly have any left. Yet they continued to stream down her face, and she was helpless to stop them.

As the procession moved through the town gate, she was certain every bit of happiness that would ever be hers was behind her. She dreaded having to walk back to an empty house, knowing that her life could never be the same again. She wailed in agony at the very thought of it, and her fellow mourners joined with her in sympathy.

An unfamiliar voice interrupted their wailing, telling her not to cry. Although tenderness and compassion filled His voice, she could not believe anyone would dare tell her not to cry. How could she possibly keep from crying? Did He have any idea what she was going through? Who was this man who expected her to dry her tears?

As she turned to discover who had spoken to her, He walked right up to the coffin, and she wondered what He was going to do. He reached up and touched the coffin, and those who carried it stood still. Then He spoke directly to the young man as if he could hear Him, and ordered him to get up. To her astonishment, *he did!* He sat up and spoke, and the man walked him over to her, alive and well.

For a brief moment, she thought her shock and grief had caused her to hallucinate, but then hope welled up in her and she reached out and touched him. Overcome with amazement and joyful thanksgiving, she threw her arms around him and smothered him with kisses.

A hush of worshipful awe had fallen over the crowd, and then all at once they began praising God. But no one praised God more than the mother who had received her beloved son back from the dead. Tears continued to pour from her eyes, but they were now transformed into tears of joy. Some of the people said that a great prophet was among them, and that

God had come to help His people. Yes, she thought, her heart was bursting with the truth of their words.

As Jesus, His disciples and the large crowd with Him approached the town gate, a funeral procession snaked its way through it and moved toward them. While they paused to allow the large group of mourners to pass by them, His eyes fell on the woman who gave voice to her grief over the deceased. Between her wailing and sobbing, she cried out for her only son and the husband she'd lost at an earlier time. Her friends attempted to comfort her, but she could not be comforted.

As Jesus observed all this, His heart went out to her. He hated the anguish sin and death had unleashed on His children. He felt the sting of their pain and carried their sorrows in His heart. He longingly anticipated the time when His work would be accomplished and death defeated, although He knew He had much to suffer before that plan was realized. Eventually He would wipe every tear from their eyes, and death, mourning, crying, and pain would cease.

He reflected on the brief time at the beginning, in the garden, before sin entered and with it the ugliness of separation and death. A plan was formulated even before that day that, when brought to completion, would remove the curse, restore access to the tree of life, and reinstate the fellowship of the garden. But sadly, that time had not yet come. For now, He must help this poor soul who wept so dejectedly, feeling alone even while surrounded by caring people.

Most of the time He required from those who needed His intervention that they ask for help and express faith. But sometimes He chose to lavish good gifts on His children just because He loved them. And this was one of those times. This sad, lonely widow needed a touch of His love in the worst way. Lost in her sorrow, she was oblivious to His presence, and did not ask or expect Him to help her. He understood that her losses had put her faith to the severest test, and compromised her ability to believe for now.

He walked over to her and gently told her not to cry. She seemed somewhat offended by this, but He just smiled knowingly and made His way to the coffin. He touched it, and the men who carried it halted. He looked into the face of the young man and commanded him to get up. Immediately his eyes fluttered open, and he sat up and began to talk. Jesus grabbed his hand and helped him up, and walked him over to his astonished mother. For a brief moment, she just stood there with her mouth wide open, thinking she must be dreaming. Then suddenly she threw her arms around her son and hugged and kissed him repeatedly. Oh, He did love these happy reunions! It was one of His favorite things about His ministry.

His thoughts turned to another reunion that He would bring about later on between a brother and his two sisters, who were dear friends of His. He reflected on the many souls who would come to faith in Him as a result, but realized that it would precipitate a crisis for the ones who insisted on rejecting Him, setting in motion His suffering and death. Then the morning would dawn when He would be the one who sat up, walked out of a tomb, and had a joyful reunion with a woman whose eyes were full of tears. That reunion would take place *in a garden.* (John 20:11-18) All these things were planned long ago to restore the life of the garden that sin had corrupted.

He would be so glad when it was all behind Him and eternity with all of His loved ones stretched out before Him. He anticipated that time with great joy and satisfaction. Suddenly the words of praise and gratitude the people uttered brought Him out of His reverie and back to the present. The words on their lips brought a smile to His face. Yes, my children, He thought, that's right. God has come to help His people, and He's delighted to do it.

Take a closer look:
1. Read Luke 7:11-17, Hebrews 4:13-16 & Psalm 34:18. What can you learn from these Scriptures about God's heart for those who grieve?
2. Read Isaiah 61:1-3 & Luke 4:16-21. Would you say that Jesus' mission statement for His ministry is summarized in these passages? What can we learn from this to help us minister to one another?
3. Read Genesis 2:8-3:24; Isaiah 25:7-9; Revelation 21:3-5 & 22:1-5. How did sin and death enter the world, and how will they be abolished?
4. Read Romans 12:15 & 2 Corinthians 1:3-7. Why does God allow Christians to experience

tragedy? What does He want us to learn from it?

5. Have you suffered the loss of a loved one? List ways that people helped and comforted you. Then list things that were said or done that were not helpful or that were even hurtful. If you have not yet experienced this, ask someone who has been through loss how others helped them. What did you learn that would enable you to better offer comfort to the grieving?

CHAPTER 6

A Husband Hopper

The dust swirled at her feet as she strode briskly along, and colored the hem of her dress. Atop her head she carried a water jar, which nearly toppled off when she swatted at a gnat that insistently buzzed about her face. Adding to her annoyance, she noticed a man sitting by the well. From His appearance, she surmised that He was a Jew. Oh great, she thought to herself, I avoided the morning rush for water, and the scorn of the neighbor women, only to be belittled by a Jewish man.

Most Jews she had ever encountered seemed to think Samaritans were inferior to them. In fact, they avoided traveling through Samaria if they could, lest they be contaminated or something. And she was pretty disillusioned with men in general. She had failed at so many marriages that she had given up on marriage, and moved in with the current man in her life without bothering to marry him. Why should she, when she expected him to tire of her and abandon her anyway, after the newness wore off and he found out how unlovable she was. It happened every time. She had long since learned not to hope for anything better; it hurt too much when the disappointment came. She had resigned herself to enjoy love while it lasted, and move on when it faded away.

For now, she must replenish her water supply. She stuffed her annoyance inside, and proceeded to the well. A friendly smile radiated from the man's face and caught her off guard. Then He politely asked her for a drink. Without stopping to think, she blurted out her surprise that a Jew would talk to a Samaritan woman, let alone ask for a drink from her hand. He replied that if she knew the gift of God, and who it was that asked her for a drink, she would have asked Him, and He would have given her living water. She wondered what He meant by "living water", but instead of asking Him to explain, she questioned where He could get this living water, seeing He had nothing to draw with and the well was deep. Was He greater than their ancestor Jacob (a subtle reminder, she thought, that Samaritans were descended from Jacob too, not just the Jews), who had provided the well for himself, his sons and his flocks and herds? He replied that everyone who drank from that well would thirst again, but whoever drank the water He gave them would never thirst. He further explained that the water He offered would produce in the one who drank it a spring of water welling up to eternal life.

She began to wonder who this man was. She struggled to understand His meaning about the water, but the thought of living without thirst and without having to come to the well to draw water appealed to her. So for those reasons she asked Him to give her some. He produced no water, but instead told her to go get her husband and come back. Why did He have to bring that up, and where was the water He said He would give her if she asked?

She told Him she had no husband. He agreed, and revealed that He knew about all five of her former husbands, and that she now had a man who was not her husband. He commended her for speaking the truth.

Her curiosity was fully aroused as to who this man was and how He knew so much about her. She studied His face more carefully, but concluded that she had never seen Him before. Who could have told Him so many details about her life, and why? Perhaps He was a fortuneteller or wizard or something.

Then the realization dawned on her that maybe He was a prophet. The idea made her very uncomfortable. She intentionally avoided religious people; they reminded her too much of her shortcomings. But it occurred to her that if she brought up some religious topic and engaged Him in a discussion about it, maybe it would divert His attention away from her failures. She said, "Sir, I can see that you are a prophet." Then she launched into the subject of whether worshippers must go to Jerusalem as the Jews claimed, or could worship on this mountain as her ancestors did.

He replied that the time was coming when the emphasis of worship would not be about a particular place, but about knowing the Father they worshipped.

He explained that Samaritans didn't know what they worshipped, but the Jews worshipped what they knew. And one of the things they knew was that salvation would come from their lineage. She supposed He meant the Messiah the Jews were expecting to be born to a Jewish woman eventually. He further instructed her about worshipping in spirit and in truth, and how the Father desired that kind of worshippers.

She did not fully grasp what He said, but her thoughts returned to the subject of the coming Messiah. She supposed that when He came, He would explain everything to them. He plainly declared that He, the very man who spoke to her, was the Messiah.

Before she had a chance to process that declaration, a group of men coming from the direction of town interrupted them. She could see that they knew Him, and that they had not expected to find Him talking to anyone. They had apparently gone to town to buy food, because they began to show Him what they had brought Him to eat.

She hated to leave, but He must be hungry. Besides, she needed to digest the things He said to her. Her confused thoughts swirled around in her head, and she completely forgot to take her water jar as she started back to town. Was He really the Messiah? He spoke with authority about religious ideas. He knew about her without anyone telling Him. But her previous experiences with religious people had not been like that one. He hadn't belittled her, ignored her or looked at her with disdain. She had even enjoyed the conversation with Him. She liked the way He treated her with respect and dignity, instead of as an inferior. She hoped for another opportunity to hear more of what He had to say and experience more of that special treatment. Besides, He still hadn't given her that water He promised. Then again, she felt an unusual sense of satisfaction just from the brief time she had spent with Him. Was that what he meant about not thirsting? She had to tell the townspeople about this man. Would they agree that he could be the Messiah?

The journey back to Galilee had tired Jesus, and He wanted to rest. The disciples were intent on getting something to eat, so He sent them to town while He sat down to relax. Besides, He had an appointment to keep. Ah, there she was now, with her water jar precariously perched on her head. A gnat harassed her, and she impatiently swatted at it. He was aware that she had hoped to be alone at the well, and that His presence also annoyed her. Nevertheless, He was not going anywhere until His business with her was finished.

When she reached the well, He asked her to give Him a drink. Her reply exposed the cynicism that her life experiences had produced in her heart. He knew she had not enjoyed an easy, comfortable life, and He intended to offer her the only thing that could fill the void in her heart—the living water that would become a spring welling up to eternal life (John 4:13). As He almost always did, He presented His offer with pictures that He skillfully painted with words. And like many of His hearers, she was confused by the word pictures and missed the point of them. She focused on the well and the liquid contained in it, while He referred to the spiritual water that cleansed, purified, refreshed and infused life into the spirits of those who chose to partake of it.

Before this one could make that choice, He must free her by breaking down the walls she had built to protect her heart. Her walls had instead imprisoned her, and bound her to her past. He had attracted her attention with His talk of living water, and instilled in her a curiosity to find out more and a desire to receive it. He had accomplished the first step.

Now to begin the demolition of the walls she thought hid her, He told her to go call her husband and come back. Her face instantly wore a troubled expression, and she denied having a husband. He commended her honesty, and divulged to her His knowledge of her five previous husbands and her current living situation. She squirmed under His scrutiny, but His insight into her life intrigued her.

Uncomfortable with the direction of the conversation, she attempted to change the subject, moving it from the personal to the general. She brought up what she thought would be a controversial issue that could generate a lengthy discussion and divert Him away from her personal problems—whether the Jews or the Samaritans were right about where to worship.

Her tactics presented no problem for Him. He simply used it as a springboard to better acquaint her with the Father she searched for in all the wrong places. He introduced her to concepts that took her in a completely new direction. First He explained that the advantage the Jews possessed was their knowledge, and one thing they knew was that salvation was coming from them. He went on to say that the time had come when the focus must turn from externals, such as location, ritual or tradition. They had never been the priority in the Father's mind. The Father sought worshippers that knew Him and whose spirits were knitted together with His, who truly worshipped Him with their minds, hearts and spirits.

As she began to process His words in her mind, the mention of salvation coming from the Jews sparked a thought about the Messiah. She expressed her certainty that the Messiah was coming, and that He would explain everything. Clearly, she struggled to comprehend what He had said.

He knocked down the last few bricks in her wall with His next words. He told her that the Messiah she expected was standing right in front of her. She blinked her eyes in astonishment, but before the words sunk in, the disciples returned and brought the conversation to an abrupt halt.

Their interruption did not bother Him at all, because He foresaw that it was only temporary. As she quickly departed, He rejoiced in the knowledge that she would experience some inner healing when she discovered that she could be a vessel in God's service in spite of her failures. In fact, He specialized in turning the very failures of His children into powerful testimony to His grace in their lives.

The townspeople she now hurried to tell of her encounter with Him would soon become thirsty to learn more about Him. Because of what they knew about her, the effect of her testimony would trigger that thirst like salt on their tongues. Their hearts would be opened, and He would be invited in to teach them further. He pictured the faces of the people whose lives were about to be forever changed, their knowledge of the Father expanded and their hearts knitted together with His, and He anticipated the coming days with great excitement. Meanwhile, He turned to His disciples. Their eyes needed to be opened to the fields around them, ripe for harvest. It promised to be a bountiful one. He must prepare the reapers.

Take a closer look:
1. Read John 4:1-42. What affects you the most in this narrative? What have you learned about God's heart for lost souls?
2. Read John 6:35 & 7:37-39; and Isaiah 44:3-4. How would you describe the living water Jesus offered, and its effects?
3. Read Matthew 5:6; Psalm 42:1-2, 63:1-5 & 107:8-9. What do our souls hunger and thirst for? What truly satisfies them?
4. Read Isaiah 55:1-2; Revelation 7:16-17, 21:6 & 22:17. What is God's offer to the thirsty?
5. Read Matthew 25:35-40. What is our responsibility to the people God brings into our lives?
6. How has God turned your failures into powerful testimony of His grace? Who are you telling about it?

CHAPTER 7

Sabbath Savior

Pain was her constant companion. Every muscle that still worked hurt. Some days were better than others, and thankfully this was one of the better days. It meant she would be able to go to synagogue, which was not always the case. Sabbaths were easier days, since the only effort she had to put forth was the short walk to the synagogue. But when the pain intensified, those few steps seemed to multiply into miles, so on those days she just had to stay home and try to rest.

Even resting proved difficult most of the time, tormented as she was by muscle spasms and joints that ached constantly. She barely remembered how it felt to wake up refreshed and rested from a good night's sleep. She survived on whatever brief naps her body afforded her, and did the best she could in her fatigued state.

Everyday tasks loomed over her in monstrous proportions. Before she was afflicted with this crippling malady, she whizzed through them practically without a thought. Many years had passed since she moved like that, swiftly and comfortably. Now the smallest task required monumental effort and a ridiculous amount of time. If she had known what a wonderful blessing of good health she took for granted back then, her heart would have overflowed with gratitude to God.

She wondered if her affliction was God's punishment for her lack of gratitude, or maybe some other sin, since her many tearful prayers went unanswered. She sighed deeply as she pondered these things, and hobbled along to the synagogue. She needed an encouraging word, and hoped the rabbi would deliver one today.

Upon arrival, she searched with some difficulty for a place to sit where she could see, since she had lost the ability to sit up straight. Finally, a kind woman noticed her struggle, offered her seat on the aisle, and moved to an empty seat down the row. Slowly and carefully, she eased her fragile body down into the seat.

A hush fell over the assembly as the rabbi took His place at the front. She didn't recognize Him, and wondered who He was. He took up the scroll, read from the Scriptures, and began to teach. As He spoke, His eyes scanned the crowd, and came to rest on her. Compassion and kindness emanated from them, and warmed her weary heart. She was encouraged by the love she read in those eyes.

Then He amazed her by calling her to come forward. What in the world was this about, she wondered? Time seemed to stand still as she painstakingly made her way to where He stood. His next words utterly surprised her, and filled her with excitement and hope. He said, "Woman, you are set free from your infirmity." (Luke 13:12) As He placed His hands on her, her tight muscles instantly loosened, her frozen joints moved freely, the pain departed, and she straightened up, tall and strong! Her delight could not be contained, but flowed from her lips in a river of praises to God! What a glorious day to be alive!

Suddenly she realized that she must thank this wonderful man. When she turned to Him, the expression on His face startled her. What was wrong? Had she celebrated too boisterously? Did He really expect her to be calm after eighteen torturous years of suffering suddenly ended?

The voice of the synagogue ruler interrupted her anxious questions. He indignantly reminded the people of the Sabbath regulations, and commanded them to come on the six working days for healing, not on the Sabbath.

She was annoyed that he thought she had come to the synagogue just to be healed. She came whenever her crippled body could tolerate the effort. That's what was expected on the Sabbath. As for the healing, she hadn't even asked for it. In fact, it was the last thing she expected to happen.

She had arrived feeling oppressed and weighed down, with no optimism that anything would ever change. She now anticipated the future with a brand-new confidence that the best days of her life had just been opened up before her. Her God took pity on her and set her free because He chose to, and she supposed He possessed the authority to do that on the Sabbath or any other day He pleased. After all, He was God. And she would rejoice and give Him glory!

The rabbi broke through these thoughts with a strong rebuke for the synagogue ruler. Then she understood that he was the one who produced the frown, and not her celebration. All distressing thoughts evaporated from her mind when the rabbi defended her as a daughter of Abraham, more important than the oxen or donkeys that were led to water every Sabbath. He justified setting her free from eighteen long years of Satan's bondage on the Sabbath day; it was appropriate that she received rest from her misery on the day God had given them for rest.

Her heart soared, feeling as light as a feather, as she looked forward to sleeping peacefully again. But that would probably be delayed until another night. As overjoyed as she felt, she doubted she would be calm enough to sleep any time soon.

Jesus' eyes came to rest on the woman, and immediately He changed the direction of His message. It was time to teach with actions rather than mere words. He realized she had endured relentless pain for many years, and decided she'd had enough. His heart ached for her, and He'd had enough as well. It was time to put Satan in his place, and free her from the hold he had ruthlessly imposed on her.

Besides all that, He'd had enough of the blindness of the religious leaders, who chose to ignore the needs of the people right under their noses. Their myopic vision was centered entirely on their own interpretations of the law and their traditions they so boldly attached to it, as if God Himself had given them permission. If only they would interpret the law by the principles of goodwill and love that God intended for the law to facilitate, they might come closer to getting it right. Then they'd *see* the widow who struggled to make ends meet, the fatherless child who needed to be nurtured, the wayward prodigal who longed for mercy, and the sick and wounded who required tender care. Instead they took it upon themselves to be the Protectors and Defenders of Truth and Righteousness. Why did they think God was so weak and small He required mortals to handle that task for Him? How could they so easily dismiss the responsibilities He had clearly laid out for them? Which of them ever took it upon themselves to loose the chains of injustice, to set the oppressed free, to bind up the brokenhearted? Who cared enough to share their food with the hungry, to provide the poor wanderer with shelter or to clothe the naked? Who thought to even turn their eyes toward their own flesh and blood to catch the slightest glimpse of what they needed? (Isaiah 58:6-7)

Obviously, this was a good time for a visual demonstration of the Father's priorities. He beckoned her to come forward so that everyone could have a clear view and not miss the lesson. While He waited for her, He stood quietly. The time required for her to shuffle to the front forced them all to take a long, hard look at her. Please, my children, notice *a person,* with feelings, cares, needs and dreams just like you have. She has been here all along, but all you perceived was a "cripple".

With a word from His lips and a touch of His hand, that description fit her no longer. Like a wilted flower under a gentle rain, she stood up tall and strong and beautiful. Praise burst forth from her lips, and her joy reflected on the faces of many in the crowd, His included.

Unfortunately, every crowd seems to include at least one person who feels constrained to choke the life out of the celebration. On this occasion, the synagogue ruler volunteered for the role. His indignation for the perceived breaking of the Sabbath and his refusal to show the tiniest bit of compassion for this woman infuriated Jesus. What hypocrisy!

Every one of them thought nothing of it when they untied their donkeys and oxen and led them to water, every Sabbath day of every year of their lives. Could they honestly believe the Father permitted them to tend to their brute beasts and not to His daughters and sons?

The Father instituted the Sabbath as a *gift* to His children, a gift of time, to give their bodies a chance to rest and their spirits an opportunity to reflect and refocus. He meant for the gift to be one they shared with Him as well. He desired the day to be devoted to Him for worship, remembrance of His work in their lives, and fellowship with Him.

Their failure to understand the nature of His gift had twisted it into a noose wrapped so tightly around the necks of the people that they scarcely allowed them to breathe on the Sabbath. Instead of being restorative, they had made it oppressive.

Now a precious daughter of Abraham stood before them, giving Jesus a perfect opportunity to paint them a living picture of the Sabbath-gift. She had labored under the heavy burden of her affliction for eighteen years without a respite. He knew no better time than the Sabbath for Him to lift the weight of it from her weary shoulders and give her rest.

He perceived the humiliation His opponents felt, and willed them to allow it to prick their consciences and open their eyes and ears to see and to hear. The choice was theirs. He turned then to the people who were delighted with His works, and to the woman who continued to rejoice and glorify God. He had more celebrating to do with them, and more to teach them. It was time to get on with it.

Take a closer look:
1. Read Luke 13:10-17; Luke 6:1-11; Mark 2:27-28 & 3:1-6. How did Jesus' knowledge of Sabbath expectations differ from the Jewish leaders' understanding of them?
2. Read Matthew 13:14-15 & 15:1-9. What was Jesus' diagnosis of their problem?
3. Read Isaiah 1:11-20, 58:1-14; Matthew 25:34-40 & Mark 12:29-34. What has God said His priorities are? Does He place more importance on some commandments than He does on others? Have we focused on the right things?

4. Read Exodus 20:8-11, 23:10-12 & 31:12-17;
    Leviticus 23:3 & 25:1-22. List all the ways
    that God described the Sabbath.
5. Read Matthew 11:28-30 & Hebrews 4:1-16.
    What is our Sabbath-rest?
6. Read Job 1:6-2:10; Luke 13:16; 2 Corinthians
    4:7-11, 16-18 & 12:7-10; James 1:2-4; & 1
    Peter 5:8-10. Why does God allow suffering
    in this world?

CHAPTER 8

Arrogance Annihilated

S he could not believe what was happening to her. She'd never been so ashamed and embarrassed. If she could just disappear and never be seen again, she would. But there she was, naked except for the sheet she'd managed to grab, being dragged through town in full view of everyone. The man who had been so sweet and tender just moments before had suddenly turned on her and yanked her out of the bed and into the street. Several other men were waiting just outside the door to join him in this ghastly parade.

Why was he treating her this way? She thought he cared for her, but apparently he had been putting on an act. Why had she fallen for it? Oh, what would her husband say when he found out? What would he do? She doubted his feelings would be hurt, since he hardly seemed to care about her anyway, but probably his pride would suffer. He would most likely cast her off like so much rubbish. Then what would she do to survive?

All at once, she tuned in to what her captors were saying, and realized her very survival was about to be decided. She was nothing but a pawn in a trap for a man named Jesus. They were discussing confidently how they surely had Him this time. He had to uphold the Law, which said she must be stoned as an adulteress. If He let her go, they could accuse Him of breaking the Law. They knew Him well enough to know He would want to let her go. Sneering disgustedly, they agreed that He always chose her kind as friends and companions. They couldn't wait to see Him unsuccessfully try to weasel out of the situation, so they could accuse Him of being a fraud. They had already decided He was one, but they wanted to persuade the people who so naively believed in Him.

They had set a trap for her then, in order to use her to bait their trap for Him. She could scarcely believe how easily she had fallen into it. Everything seemed innocent enough at the beginning. It started with a friendly smile as she walked to the market. She knew the man as a business associate of her husband, so it was not unusual for her to see him around town. What she failed to notice was how he subtly began to appear along her path more and more frequently.

One day someone bumped against her and some of her purchases fell out of her basket. As she struggled to round them up and put them back in, there he was to help her. They had a brief chat and went their separate ways. The next time she saw him, the dialogue continued a little longer, and following conversations grew longer still.

Soon she found herself hoping to see him every time she went out. At the same time, she dreaded the guilt she felt every time she realized that he was becoming more important to her than her husband was. Because her husband rarely spent time with her or conversed with her, she felt lonely, unattractive and unloved. After a lonely childhood wishing her father would pay attention to her, she had hoped things would be different once she married.

At one time, she had freely given her father affection, and chattered happily to him about whatever came to her mind. Rather than returning her affection, he behaved as if she were a nuisance to him. One day she realized he was ignoring her endless chatter, and she stopped sharing her heart with him. He completely broke her heart when he failed to notice or to miss her.

When she married, she hoped to be such a good wife that she could win her husband's interest and affection. Instead, the void inside her only grew deeper and wider. He spent countless hours away from home, and when he was there, his mind was occupied elsewhere. She often wondered what was wrong with her, that she never seemed to be able to attract anyone's attention or affection.

That is, until this other man came into her life. He made her feel special and attractive. He took an interest in her activities and feelings. He listened to what she had to say, and shared his thoughts with her. She sensed that she was heading into dangerous territory, but that very danger brought with it an excitement that she found exhilarating. The more she realized she ought to pull away from him, the more she felt drawn to him.

Then one day while her husband was out, he came to her back door and asked to come in. They chatted briefly, as she went about her household tasks. Suddenly she sensed his nearness, and as she turned to look at him, he wrapped his arms around her and kissed her. His kiss both terrified and electrified her. She knew she ought to immediately run far away from him and never look back, but her good sense forsook her and she let her feelings take over.

She began living for the times when they were together, and rationalizing the guilt that threatened to swallow her up. Her husband's inattention made it effortless to slip away and easy to make excuses in her own mind. So things had transpired until this day when things suddenly, dreadfully changed. Now the man and his cohorts were humiliating her publicly and subjecting her to a possible death by stoning. What happened to the tender, attentive, and affectionate man she thought she had finally found? Obviously, he was none of those things in reality. He was nothing but a user, and she felt like such a loser.

They found the target of their ire and shoved her in front of Him. Having finally let go of her, she tried to huddle down and hide herself with the sheet. They wouldn't permit it, but forced her to stand and face the gathered crowd. They accused her of adultery, saying they had caught her in the act. What hypocrites! She hadn't committed adultery by herself, but they said nothing about the man who participated in it with her. At this moment she realized he had seduced her into it, but he certainly didn't make any move to come forward and confess to his part in the transgression. The man she thought she had fallen in love with she now found she hated even more.

Her accusers declared that Moses commanded such women must be stoned. What does He say? She hardly breathed while she waited for His response. On one hand, if they killed her she'd never have to face her husband who had yet to find out or the townspeople who had already learned of her misdeeds. On the other hand, she dreaded the pain the stones would inflict on her body, however briefly. She knew as well that she was in no position to stand before her Maker and account for herself.

Her apprehension intensified as the rabbi remained silent. Instead of speaking, He bent over and wrote on the ground with His finger. She assumed He had to weigh whether to sacrifice her to save Himself, or sacrifice His own reputation to save her.

The men who had set this trap for Him kept pressing him for an answer. They were, however, totally unprepared for what He had to say when He finally stood up and opened His mouth. Their trap melted away into nothingness when He stated that whoever was without sin could be the first to cast a stone at her. Then He stooped back down and continued to write on the ground.

She was amazed and relieved as, one by one, forced to admit his own sinful state, each one walked away. She stood alone before Him, frozen to the spot, and waited to see what He would do next. Straightening Himself up, He looked directly into her eyes and asked where her accusers were. Had no one condemned her? When she said no one had, He told her He didn't either. Then He told her she was free to go and leave her life of sin behind.

She could hardly believe her ears, but her eyes had caught a glimpse of mercy and love when she looked into His. Somehow her heart felt full for the first time since she was very young, while at the same time so light she almost believed she could fly. She sensed that she'd been in the very presence of God, and that He had forgiven her of her sins. To her amazement, He loved her in spite of what she had done.

She still had to face her husband, and could not predict how he would deal with her. Whatever her future held, she determined that she would hold onto the love and mercy she had discovered that day. She would walk in the light of that love as long as she lived. Whenever she experienced loneliness or rejection, she would remind herself who she was, a beloved child of her Father in heaven.

As far as he was concerned, Jesus of Nazareth was the most exasperating person on the face of the earth. He was sick and tired of the humiliation he suffered in front of other people because of Him. What made Him think He knew so much about the law anyway? Did He ever sit at the feet of any rabbi to partake of his teaching? He didn't think so, yet He was so authoritative about it, offending men like him who had been students of the law since their youth and teachers of it as adults.

Somehow, He always made them look like fools, the way He twisted things around to His advantage. He added to their frustration by impressing so many people with His trickery. By the time this rebel finished tampering with it, he did not know what would become of their religion. Why, He regularly violated the Sabbath regulations and then defended His actions by claiming to be Lord of the Sabbath. What blasphemy! In addition, He blasphemed by professing to be the son of God, come down from heaven! What an unbelievable claim, since they knew He was the son of Joseph and his wife.

They had to do something about Him, but every time they tried to trip Him up, He wriggled out of it and made them look bad instead. This time they had Him, though. There was no way He could get out of the trap they planned for Him. They knew how much He loved sinners, so all they had to do was make Him choose between the law and a sinner. Whatever choice He made, He would lose. Then the people would see that either Jesus was no authority on the law or that He did not love them as much as He claimed.

The plan was foolproof. They'd come up with it weeks ago, and patiently waited until the trap was set. His role in the scheme was to capture the bait. He had to catch someone committing a heinous sin, and when that never materialized, he decided to ensnare some vulnerable soul in it himself.

He studied the women in the marketplace until he found one who looked lonely and hungry for attention. All he had to do was give her what she craved, and she'd be all his. His plan required him to violate the law himself, but for the good of the cause, he was willing to do it. If he could enjoy some pleasure along the way, then why shouldn't he?

Before long, he detected the look he sought in a woman he recognized as the wife of a business associate. He knew her husband stayed so preoccupied with his business, she'd be easy to lead astray, and her husband would never notice until it was too late to prevent it. When he learned she made an effort to live morally, he moved slowly and carefully to avoid arousing any misgivings in her. He played his role to perfection, and won her trust, then her love, and finally her body.

After taking advantage of her until he had his fill, he informed his cohorts that the time had come. He arranged for them to find out where Jesus was on this particular day, and then come to his house and wait for him outside. She willingly answered his summons, and he seduced her without difficulty. He felt a twinge of remorse knowing how he had used her, but eased his conscience by telling himself it was her own fault for being so weak and gullible. Once he heard the others outside, he yanked her up and dragged her outside.

She alternated between struggling to free herself and attempting to cover herself with the sheet she had managed to grab. Between clenched teeth, she asked why, expressed her hurt, and spit out her sudden hate of him. He was too busy manhandling her to bother to answer. Besides he was thinking about the triumph he expected to enjoy soon over that irksome Jesus. The sight of her being dragged along the streets attracted a large crowd, much to his delight. The more present the better, to witness Jesus' downfall.

Finally, his friends lead them to Jesus, and he shoved the adulteress toward Him. She made an effort to hide herself, but one of the others forced her to stand facing the crowd. Then another one posed the question designed to put Jesus in an inescapable dilemma. His silence pleased them, as they thought He grappled with the undesirable choices before Him. Nevertheless, when He bent down and started writing on the ground with His finger, they pressed Him for an answer.

They waited expectantly while He straightened up and opened His mouth to speak. What He said demolished any hope of conquest over Him, and silenced every one of His opponents. He said whoever was without sin among them was free to throw the first stone.

The man who had ensnared the woman in his foul plot to trap Jesus stood dumbfounded as, one by one, the others realized their guilty state and slowly went away. At first, he fought against his conscience, but eventually he had to give in to its insistence. As he slowly staggered away under the heaviness of his shame, he marveled at Jesus' ability to elude every effort to destroy His influence or do away with Him. He thought he had a foolproof idea, but Jesus blew it away like so much dust. What would he have to do to rid himself of that infuriating man?

As Jesus sat down to teach the people gathered around Him, He caught a glimpse of a group of Pharisees and teachers of the law hurrying away. He knew their purpose, and was ready to deal with them when they returned. He wasted no time fretting about them, but used the time to instruct His listeners.

He had come to Jerusalem for the Feast of Tabernacles, and had spent several days teaching in the temple courts. Many had come to believe in Him, while others grappled with unanswered questions. If only they would ask, He would quickly clear up their confusion. But as long as they kept their doubts to themselves, He allowed them to wrestle with them.

Most of the Pharisees and chief priests chose to continue in their stubborn unbelief. Since they were so convinced of their own knowledge of the Scriptures, they refused to consider any new perspectives or interpretations that differed from their own. Their pride would not allow them to be teachable or to open their minds and hearts to any possibility that He was who He claimed to be. Because of this, every time He substantiated His claims or shed light on their erroneous beliefs, they reacted with resentment and lashed out at Him or slipped away to plot against Him.

He realized they were planning an attempt to trip Him up at that very moment, but He was unconcerned. In just a little while, their bait and their intended prey would be making peace with one another while they were off somewhere nursing their wounded pride one more time. They would not give in no matter how many times they were publicly embarrassed or how He demonstrated His power and authority.

Eventually, He would pay a heavy price for their unbelief, but the toll exacted on them would be even higher. The thought of it tore at His heart, but He would never take away their freedom to choose or reject Him. Therefore, He patiently tolerated the attempts they made to discredit Him, arrest Him, or even to kill Him. Their time would come, but not until the Father determined it.

The latest attempt to arrest Him had failed because the temple guards they sent were open-minded enough to entertain the possibility that He was for real. Since He kept slipping through their fingers, they had devised a scheme they thought would ensnare Him without fail. It had been set in motion weeks before, and was culminating at that very moment, as they arrived back with their unfortunate victim.

With a self-righteousness that nauseated Him, they demanded that He either pronounce judgment on her for committing adultery, meaning she should be stoned to death, or implicate Himself as a lawbreaker. Never mind that the one who lured her into it, and was even more at fault than she, shamelessly stood among them accusing her as if he was innocent as a dove.

His heart overflowed with compassion for her, and He diverted all eyes away from her exposed, embarrassed figure by kneeling down and writing on the ground. He was aware they were attempting to see what He was writing. That was not the important thing, He mused, but rather what each of them had written on his own heart. What laws had they hidden in them, and which of them had they violated? That is what they needed to be asking, not what to do about the woman who was no more sinful than the rest of them.

He ignored their repeated questioning long enough to ensure that every eye was on Him, anticipating His response. Then He dropped the bombshell that forced each one to look within, face the truth they saw there, and walk away. Not one among them was sinless, qualified to throw any stones at her. He was qualified to throw them, but once again, His thoughts turned to the future, when He would take the nails in His hands rather than stones.

Meanwhile, He focused on the woman and considered what had gone wrong in her life. He was well acquainted with temptation, and understood its powerful pull toward sin. He sympathized with her weakness (Heb. 4:15), knowing that neglect by the two most important men in her life had left her heart hungry and vulnerable. Where she had failed was in guarding her heart and controlling her thoughts (Proverbs 4:23). Because every sin begins with a thought, He knew the battle against it must be fought and won in the mind before ever coming to the point of taking action with the body (2 Corinthians 10:3-5). The hunger of her heart needed to find satisfaction by partaking of the bread of life, rather than in human relationships.

Only the Father could fill her emptiness, because sin had not weakened or blinded His heart as it had the hearts of her earthly father and her husband. He would keep His promises to be a husband to the widow and a Father to the fatherless. She was not fatherless or a widow in the truest sense of the words, because her father and husband lived, but both failed to be present for her. Nevertheless, the Father would faithfully nurture her heart if she ran to Him rather than to faithless, fallen men.

He was the source of power that would infuse her heart with the strength to stand against temptation and maintain her purity. Although she had surrendered her purity and stained her heart, He intended to cleanse and restore her. He specialized and delighted in brand new beginnings, and the precious one who stood trembling before Him was in dire need of one.

She could have easily fled the minute all the others had departed, but instead she remained rooted to the ground on which she stood. When He rose and looked into her eyes, He saw the fear and dread of a condemned criminal awaiting her sentence. He loved watching her expression transformed into relief and hope as He assured her that He didn't condemn her. She was free to go and leave her sin behind.

She departed from His presence with lightheartedness, coupled with a resolute determination to do just as He said. He moved on with the deep sense of satisfaction born of fulfilling His purpose for living. What a great feeling that was!

Take a closer look:
1. Read John 8:1-11. Did Jesus violate the Law of Moses? Did He condone the woman's adultery? How would Jesus' words benefit her as she went on her way?

2. Read Leviticus 20:10 & Deuteronomy 22:22. What did the Law of Moses command concerning adultery?

3. Read Psalms 10:14; 68:4-6; 146:3-9; & Isaiah 54:4-6. What are the Lord's promises for the lonely?

4. Read Psalm 145:8-9 & 13b-19; Isaiah 1:18-20, 53:5-6, 11-12; 54:7-10; & 55:6-7. How does the Lord describe Himself? What are His promises to those who have sinned?

5. Read 1 Corinthians 6:9-20. What sins had the Corinthians committed before their conversion? What had Christ done for them? What makes adultery and other sexual sins so wrong?

6. Read 1 Corinthians 10:6-13. What is the warning in this passage? What specific things can you do to protect yourself from falling into sexual sins?

7. Read Romans 2:1-24; 3:10-12 & 21-26; 5:6-11; 7:21-8:2; 8:31-39; 12:1-2 & 13:12-14. Who is truly righteous? What is the remedy for sin?

8. Read Hebrews 2:14-18; 4:14-16; 7:24-27; 8:10-12; 9:13-14; 10:19-23 & 13:4-6. How has Jesus fulfilled the Old Testament promises for sinful people?

CHAPTER 9

Sibling Struggles

She bustled about her kitchen in a whirlwind of activity. Freshly baked bread was nestled in a basket near the oven to keep warm. Inside the oven, the meat roasted, seasoned with her own special blend of fresh herbs and brushed with oil. She fretted as she mentally inventoried the things she had yet to do. She wanted everything to be just right for their honored guest. He was very dear to her heart, as well as to her sister's and brother's.

She enjoyed the role of hostess, although she brought a good bit of stress on herself with her perfectionism. She always thoroughly exhausted herself by the time her guests departed, and resolved to do things less elaborately in the future. However, by the next time, she forgot her fatigue and her resolve melted away, and she threw herself into the same flurry of activity as before.

When someone as special as Jesus was among the guests, she put even more demands on herself to create an exceptional banquet. His arrival in town was unexpected, but she wasted no time extending Him an invitation to visit in her home. Immediately she set to work to prepare a fine feast for Him. When He appeared at the door long before her preparations were completed, she let her sister go to the door to welcome Him in, and greeted Him briefly before returning to her tasks with an even greater urgency.

Vegetables and fruits awaited washing and preparing, rooms required tidying and sweeping, she had yet to clean the kitchen up from the bread making, and she still wanted to go out and gather some fresh flowers for a centerpiece. In addition, the bowls for hand washing needed filling and towels set out, and the dishes set around the table.

Where was Mary, and why did she not help her with all this work? Every time she needed assistance, she had to go searching for Mary. She always found her daydreaming or engaged in conversation, oblivious to the necessary tasks that kept the household running smoothly.

Both of her siblings depended on Martha to take care of everything. She was quickly running out of patience, under the pressures of the moment as well as all the responsibilities expected of her. Just once, she wished one of them would volunteer to help her. So many details screamed out to her for attention, and she wondered how they could fail to notice them as well. What Martha found completely obvious was lost on her siblings. Besides, she was convinced that what they failed to notice, they also neglected to appreciate. Not only did Martha have to take care of everything, they took her for granted as well. While they visited with the guests, she slaved away with all the serving. Did they ever consider that she might enjoy relaxing and enjoying the company of their visitors occasionally? Of course they never did. Well, she had all she could take of that and refused to stand for it another minute. She marched into the other room and asked Jesus if He cared that her sister left her with all the work, and demanded that He tell her to help.

Disconcerted by His reply, she meekly resumed her activity while she considered His words. He said only one thing was important, and not all the many things she worried and fumed over. Mary had made the better choice, and He declined to take it away from her. Did He really mean to say all her efforts were unimportant? Did He not realize she did them for Him? Furthermore, if she didn't prepare the meal and see to everything, who would? How long before the entire household descended into chaos, if she sat down and left it to someone else? Was there a middle ground she had failed to discern in all her busyness?

She reflected on how many resolutions she had made to simplify, and how quickly she had forgotten them. Perhaps she set her standards a little too high in regards to her homemaking. If she loosened her objective from perfection to sufficiency, would her world immediately fall apart? By simplifying, how much time would open up for her to sit at Jesus' feet as Mary did? What frustration had she brought upon herself by her stringent expectations? Memories came to mind of instances when Mary had tried to help, but because Martha wanted it done a certain way, she gave her criticism rather than gratitude. No wonder she never volunteered any more, she thought remorsefully.

As she called everyone to the table and served the meal, she remained pensive and quiet. She studied her sister and brother with new perceptiveness. For the first time, she took notice of vast differences in each of their personalities. Mary had always been more of a thinker than a doer. Lazarus saw everything differently than either of the sisters. Details that Martha could not ignore, the other two never perceived. She must learn to accept and enjoy their differences, instead of expecting them to be copies of her.

Her eyes also opened that day to her responsibility to ask politely for their assistance on specific tasks. Then she must allow them to do those tasks without her disapproval of their methods, and express appreciation for their efforts. It had dawned on her that in the past, she had stewed about their negligence until her temper flared, and then angrily demanded action from them. Another tactic she used was to play the martyr until guilt moved them to action. Neither of those methods had been effective, but instead left everyone feeling upset and resentful.

She determined never to do those things again, knowing it would require all the strength she could muster to keep herself in check. Along those lines, she resolved once again to keep things simple and desperately hoped she had finally learned that lesson.

Mary awaited Jesus' arrival with eager anticipation. She was delighted when Martha told her He was coming. She had so many pleasant memories of His visits. She loved to sit at His feet and soak in His teachings. His words nourished her spirit and stimulated her mind, leaving her with much to digest long after He went on His way. She thrived on intellectual stimulation and spiritual discourse, and no one provided such things as well as Jesus did.

Lost in these thoughts, the knock at the door startled her. She quickly jumped up and ran to the door to greet Him and welcome Him in. Since the meal was not quite ready, she offered Him a seat and positioned herself at His feet. It never occurred to her to go and help with the preparations, so intent was she on conversing with their guest. Jesus immediately began feeding the bread of life to her receptive heart, and there arose within her the deep satisfaction His teachings gave her.

They were unaware of the passage of time until Martha's sharp voice penetrated the air. Mary immediately felt remorseful for neglecting to help her sister, a feeling that troubled her often. Martha was so often already upset before the thought even occurred to Mary to help her. She realized by that time her aid meant far less to her sister than if she had volunteered it earlier. Still, she would jump up and hurry to find out what Martha wanted her to do, and meekly try to fulfill her wishes. Often she only irritated her further by failing to do things the way she wanted them done, giving her the feeling she was only getting in the way of progress. Whatever she did, it seemed she could not win.

She never intentionally refused to contribute; her mind was always on other things. Her sister was the one to notice all the little details and attend to them. Mary marveled at her efficiency and her competency to manage things so well. She felt clumsy and inadequate by comparison. She wished she had just half the energy and organizational skills that came so naturally to Martha. No matter how hard she tried to be like her, she was entirely different. Now she had offended her once again.

When Martha blew into the room and voiced her complaint, Jesus' words stopped her just as she was about to jump up and run as she normally did. He said the many things Martha fretted about were unnecessary. Only one thing mattered, and Mary had chosen it. He refused to take it away from her. She saw that His response stunned Martha, and she went back to work without a word.

Mary resolved to discuss these things with her later, unsure whether she understood all that He had said herself. Did He mean keeping the house in order and preparation of meals was unnecessary? Someone had to do those things, did they not? Was there a way that she and Martha could work together and find a better balance between spiritual pursuits and household responsibilities? Was Martha envious of the time she spent visiting with their guest?

Mary thought she went to so much trouble because she enjoyed it, but maybe she felt duty-bound to do it. Did she ever tell her how much she appreciated everything she did for the family, or keep it to herself as often as she thought about it? Did Martha have any idea how much she admired her and wished to be more like her? Or how bad she felt when she disappointed her? Had she taken her too much for granted?

She determined to have a conversation with her sister concerning these questions at the first opportunity. Meanwhile, the realization dawned on her that Jesus had commended her choice to sit at His feet listening to what He said. Nothing pleased her more than to know she had pleased the Master, and she was thrilled that He enjoyed their time together as much as she did.

Jesus was tired from traveling and hungry as well. He gladly accepted Martha's invitation to dine in her home. His visits with them were always enjoyable. Martha prepared wonderful meals, Lazarus welcomed His friendship, and Mary embraced His teachings with a receptive ear. He knew they all loved Him dearly, and of course, He loved them even more than they could comprehend. He wished more people were like them, so open to His teaching, so trusting of Him, so devoted to Him. He sighed deeply when He thought about the many souls who would reject Him no matter what it cost them, and they would never realize the cost until it was too late. Nevertheless, He would drink in this moment, and the sweet fellowship that the evening promised to bring.

He knocked on the door, and Mary eagerly welcomed Him in. Martha stepped in for a quick greeting, and then hurried back to her kitchen to make ready their dinner. As much as He enjoyed the fine meals she created, He would have been just as happy to share a loaf of bread and a little wine with them. Martha would then be free just to sit with Him and enjoy the fellowship with the rest of them. She had no way of knowing what she missed, because she never stopped moving long enough to find out. He understood Martha showed her love by doing things for the object of her love, but sometimes He preferred being with Him over doing for Him. He could bring such clarity to her vision if she would just take a seat and listen for a while.

She desperately needed to catch a glimpse of how quickly occasions such as this passed, and learn to seize them before they slipped away. Before many more days transpired, a rude awakening awaited her as to how much her brother Lazarus meant to her. Not long after, He would go back to the Father and she would regret the opportunities to fellowship with Him she had lost. She had her priorities confused, placing so much importance on things that would never last and taking for granted the people living there with her.

She thought she knew them well, but He knew that she had not taken a discerning look at either of them in years. They were unique individuals, all three of them, and could enrich one another's lives in so many ways if they really knew and appreciated each other the way He knew them. He took pleasure in each one-of-a-kind person He created, individually selecting and blending the facets of personality that He combined to give each one their own distinct identity. If only His children would pay more attention to one another and celebrate all the differences He designed into them to make each one unique. What blessings might be theirs, what unity might they attain, what good might they accomplish together if they would each contribute the strengths of their personalities for the good of all? Instead, they judged differences in one another as character flaws or imperfections and tried to fit one another into their own molds.

Sometimes they carried unnecessary burdens when they tried to be just like others they admired, or when others imposed their expectations of who they should be on them. If their Creator had wanted to make them all alike, He could have. He chose instead to express His creativity in the designing of every person He made, and He took great delight in doing so. Their recognition, acceptance, understanding, even fascination with the distinctiveness of every individual would please Him so much. Rather than developing those qualities, they had a remarkable ability to overlook completely the people right in front of their faces or living in their own houses. In addition, they wasted energy and inflicted pain by trying to force one another or themselves to be a person they were not.

His thoughts focused back on Martha, a woman of action, and Mary, a spiritually minded thinker. While He dined with them, He decided to direct the conversation toward enlightening them about these things. He'd help them to see each other more clearly and open their hearts to the benefits each could bring to the family. Many lessons were theirs to discover from one another if they learned to seek them out. Meanwhile, He intended to enjoy these lovely people and the sumptuous feast that awaited Him.

Take a closer look:
1. Read Luke 10:38-42. Who are you most like, Mary or Martha? What might you learn from women who are more like the one you are not? What could you teach them?
2. Read Matthew 4:3. Comparing what Jesus said to the devil and to Martha, what does He teach us about prioritizing?
3. Read Ephesians 6:4 & Philippians 4:8. We can exasperate our children by not accepting who they are, trying to change them into someone they are not, or comparing them to others. Study each of your children, if you have them, and write down their unique qualities, strengths, and personality attributes. Then thank God for each of them. What do you need to change about the ways you interact with them? Now apply this activity to your spouse, your parents and siblings, extended family, co-workers, members of your congregation, and anyone you might be tempted to take for granted or try to change into a different person. This will take some time, so you will probably have to do this a little at a time.
4. Read 1 Corinthians 12:12-31 & Romans 12:3-10. Why did God make each of us different from everyone else?

5. Read Romans 9:20-21; Isaiah 29:16, 45:9-12 & 64:8. When we find fault with differences in people, what are we saying to our Creator?

6. Read John 17:11, 20-23; Romans 15:5-7; Ephesians 4:1-3, 11-16; Philippians 2:1-5 & Colossians 3:11-15. What importance did the Lord place on unity? How can we achieve it? Is conformity a necessity or a hindrance to unity?

7. Read Romans 8:29 & 12:2; Ephesians 5:1-2 & 1 Peter 1:14-16. Describe the kind of conformity the Lord expects of us.

CHAPTER 10

Bound for Burial

With great excitement, she made her way with Martha and Lazarus to Simon's house. Recent events had tightened the bond between her siblings and her, and she cherished every moment with them. Simon's invitation to dinner thrilled her because he was giving it to honor Jesus, who had just come back to Bethany. The repercussions of the miracle Jesus performed on their behalf had made it necessary for Him to go elsewhere for a while.

She barely contained her exhilaration when she thought back to that wonderful day a short time ago when Jesus had lifted her from the depths of despair and grief to the heights of joy and gladness. The heartbreak her family had suffered, and the wonder that Jesus performed to end it, had intensified her love for Him immeasurably. Lazarus had fallen seriously ill, and they sent for Jesus immediately. They waited expectantly for Him to appear, but every glance out the window disappointed them. While they nursed their brother, they believed healing could occur at any moment. They knew Jesus could say the word from anywhere with instantaneous results.

When Lazarus stopped breathing, hope and expectancy gave way to feelings of betrayal and abandonment. Where was Jesus when they needed Him? Why had He stayed away? Tears stung her eyes as she remembered those intensely painful feelings.

The sisters had endured Lazarus' burial and four days of mourning before Jesus finally appeared. Martha went out to meet Him first while Mary remained at home. She quickly ran to Him, however, when Martha relayed the message that He was asking for her. The friends who had come to mourn with them followed her. When she reached Him, she collapsed at His feet, and conveyed her belief that her brother would still be alive if He had been there. She observed that her tears and those of her friends troubled Him and moved Him to weep. Since He obviously cared so much, she could not understand why He had stayed away.

Then He went to the tomb and ordered the stone rolled away. He gave thanks to the Father for hearing Him as He always did. He stated His reason for saying so, which was to benefit the people so they would believe the Father had sent Him. Next, He shouted to Lazarus to come out of his grave, and out he came! Barely able to move because of the grave clothes, Jesus said to take them off and let him go.

What a celebration followed! All sadness immediately gave way to merriment. Finally, they understood that Jesus had not abandoned them, but intended all along to give their brother back to them. He had delayed in order to glorify the Father and display His power by bringing him to life again.

Many of their friends who had come to comfort them put their faith in Jesus. Others went to the Pharisees and reported what Jesus had done. Incredibly, the Pharisees ignored the evidence that clearly demonstrated His deity and started looking for ways to kill Him. Because of it, He withdrew to a quieter place for a while with His disciples.

Now that He had returned, Mary made up her mind to lavish on Him the love and gratitude she felt for all He had done for her. Realizing she had no way to do justice to what He deserved, she settled on an alabaster jar of very expensive perfume she had saved for a special occasion. What could be more special than this?

Upon arrival at Simon's house, Lazarus joined the men reclining at the table, Martha jumped right into serving, and Mary watched for an opportunity to carry out her plans. When she felt the time was right, she positioned herself behind Him and began to follow the bidding of her heart. She opened the jar and poured its fragrant contents on His head and His feet as He reclined at the table. Humbly wiping His feet with her hair, she communicated her adoration without words. The sweet aroma filled the house, in the same way His teachings had filled her heart. When she gazed into His face, He smiled His appreciation and affection for her.

The indignant voices of some of His disciples, however, spoiled the moment. They complained about the waste, saying they could have sold the perfume and used the money to help the poor. Their harsh rebuke of her actions stunned her. She never intended to neglect the poor, but to worship her Lord. She was well aware the cost was more than a year's wages; that was what motivated her to sacrifice it for Jesus. The magnitude of her regard for Him required extravagance in its demonstration. This was not about the poor, but about Him. Since it was between Jesus and her anyway, who gave them the right to criticize her for worshipping Him lavishly?

Before her irritation eclipsed the blissful reverence she had felt moments before, Jesus interrupted the grumbling voices of His disciples. He asked them why they bothered her and bid them to leave her alone. When He affirmed that she had done a beautiful thing for Him, she felt vindicated and her pleasant feelings welled up again. He went on to say the poor would always be among them, giving them opportunities to help whenever they chose. On the other hand, He was not going to remain with them. He linked the preparation of His body for burial with her anointing Him with perfume, and the thought of it saddened her deeply. Her spirits lifted again when He pronounced that everywhere His gospel reached, they would hear about what she had done. He commended her for doing what she could, and silenced the peevish voices of His disciples. Once again, His wisdom and kindheartedness reminded her why she adored Him so much, and she resumed her worship of Him.

Jesus was enjoying dinner and the company of His friends and followers. Difficult days lay ahead, and He wanted to make the most of happier times while they lasted. In addition, He found the joyful expressions on the faces of the two dear sisters gratifying. Their wholehearted enthusiasm upon seeing Him again warmed His heart.

The waiting and the weeping they had recently experienced had been painful for all of them, even Him. Though He had intended to call Lazarus out of the tomb in a very short time, He still felt the sorrows of His beloved children deeply. He had seen death all along from the eternal perspective of heaven, with the knowledge that a plan was in place for its demise. Looking at death from heaven's vantage point, the sorrows His children experienced touched Him, but knowing the glories of their future eternity with Him lessened the impact. He had felt its sting from the human perspective as well since taking on flesh. Sickness and death followed Him everywhere in His ministry, and He knew well how to give aid and comfort to wounded, broken people.

The misery He witnessed at the death of Lazarus was more difficult for Him than any other He had seen, however. For one thing, He had spent many hours in their home and felt especially close to all of them. He was also aware of their certainty that when they sent for Him, He would be there, or that He would at least say the word from afar to make Lazarus well. Hurt, betrayal, anger, and many unanswered questions compounded the agony they felt from the loss of their dear brother. He knew they felt as if they had lost their dearest friend in Him as well, because He had disappointed them so deeply.

He worked for a higher purpose than just the healing of a human body, which sometimes meant waiting endlessly, suffering miserably, and not understanding why until afterward for the ones who asked Him in faith to heal. Often the delay not only produced doubt in His goodness or power but doubt in the believer's own faith. If God said no to their prayers, maybe their faith had not been strong enough. While they wrestled with their doubts and questions, He carried them along and continued operating in their lives beyond what they could see. As their trials strengthened and refined them, He was designing blessings for them they could never have imagined.

In Lazarus' case, His supposed tardiness meant a great many more people were gathered together to witness the greatest miracle of His ministry. Consequently, a number of them came to faith in Him that day. Now destined to enjoy eternal life with Him, they were His reward for the mighty work He had done.

He was aware that because so many believed in Him that day, He would also pay a penalty for the same work. The ones who ran off to report to the Pharisees about it set in motion the events leading to His death. Knowing that His death was imminent, the grief Mary and Martha and their friends suffered that day brought to mind what His death would cause His loved ones to experience. As He pictured the faces of His mother and the other women who had followed Him and supported His ministry, His beloved disciples and closest friends, He could not help but weep. Seeing their anguish through human eyes gave Him a perspective on death different from heaven's eternal view, and it broke His heart.

His knowledge that resurrection followed soon afterward comforted and strengthened Him to move forward. His children were going to be required to suffer over Him, but after their fiery trial passed and they understood why things must happen this way, their lives would never be the same. What a difference they would soon make in the world!

The sound of a jar opening and the lovely aroma of perfume interrupted these reflections. Mary's eyes spoke volumes of her deep gratitude and boundless devotion to Him as she began anointing His head and His feet with the fragrant oil. Her worshipful humility and His delight in her expression of love knitted their spirits together in a moment of profound fellowship before the voices of dissent interrupted it.

Judas objected to her use of such expensive perfume when she could have sold it to help the poor. He proclaimed self-righteously that a year's wages could have fed many hungry people. This keeper of the moneybag did not fool Jesus, because He discerned his motivation was greed rather than concern for the poor. His thievery had not escaped Jesus' notice. The others chimed in with indignant accusations of waste and harsh rebukes.

So uninhibited, heartfelt, extravagant worship of their Lord was a waste, was it? Did they not realize He was God, and they were not? Had they grasped anything He tried to teach them? Did they have any idea how much she had pleased Him by her sacrifice?

He asked them why they bothered her and commanded them to leave her alone. Once they quieted their arrogant noise, He enlightened them to the beauty of what she had done. He reminded them that He was preparing to die on a tree for their sins, and stated that her use of the perfume prepared His body for burial.

If they truly cared for the poor, they could help them anytime (and money was only one way to do it). His time with them was in the closing stages. This woman had sought a way to convey the depth of her love, and did what she could for Him. What she had done pleased Him so much that He wanted her deeds told wherever they preached His gospel throughout the world.

Genuine worship such as she had demonstrated deserved remembrance and emulation. Meanwhile, His disciples had many lessons yet to learn, and He must make the most of the time He had left with them. For the moment, fellowship, breaking of bread, and expressions of love satisfied Him completely.

Take a closer look:
1.   Read Matthew 26:6-13; Mark 14:3-9 & John 12:1-8. What do you think motivated Mary to do what she did? How did Jesus respond to the disciples' rebuke of her?
2.   Read 2 Samuel 6:12-23. Why did Michal find fault with David? What was David's response? What consequence did she pay for

her criticism? What lesson is in this for us today?

3. Read John 11. Since He was about to raise Lazarus from the dead, why do you suppose Jesus wept?

4. Read Genesis 8:20-21; Exodus 29:18, 25, 41 & Numbers 28:2 & 29:8. What phrase did God use to describe the Old Testament sacrifices?

5. Read Ezekiel 20:41; Romans 12:1; 2 Corinthians 2:14-16; Ephesians 5:1-2; Philippians 4:18; Revelation 5:8 & 8:3-4. What is the aroma that pleases God under the new covenant? How's your fragrance?

6. Read Leviticus 19:11, 23:22, 25:25-28,35-42 &47-53, 27:8; Deuteronomy 15:7-11 & 24:10-15. What provision for the poor did God put in place under the Old Testament?

7. Read Matthew 19:21; Luke 12:32-33, 14:13, 21; Acts 2:44-45 & 4:32; Romans 15:26-27; Galatians 2:10; James 2:1-9 & 14-17. What is the New Testament plan concerning the poor? Does caring for the poor preclude worshipping the Lord from the heart?

CHAPTER 11

Mirror Mercies

She can be a difficult person to face. Her personality with its complexities, her humanity with its weaknesses, and her history with its disappointments, all intertwined into her identity can be a challenge for her to accept. If her hair is curly, she wishes it was straight, but if straight, she wants curls. Whatever the color of her eyes and hair, she probably prefers something else. She hates to see blemishes, wrinkles, age spots, scars or gray hairs appear. She always seems to see something she wants to change, and may spend a fortune and put herself through various levels of torture to do so. At the very least, she does what she can with hairbrush and perhaps makeup and jewelry, working with what she has to look her best.

While checking her appearance might carry some degree of discontentment with it, looking into her eyes and asking what lies behind them can be almost impossible for her to do. Who is she? What makes her tick? She wonders what she is worth and whether she is lovable. Why was she born? What difference is her life making?

She can see that she is "becoming her mother", finding the characteristics she promised herself not to emulate more readily apparent than the ones she admires. She has her father's eyes, seeing both the tenderness and love that drew her to him and the anger that frightened her away from him. She is a mixed bag of personality traits and facial features inherited from her family, some she takes pride in and others she would prefer to hide.

What emotional scars hide behind those eyes? She carries some resentment in her heart for things done to her over which she had no control. Her childhood was not easy, and she struggles to put it behind her. She definitely regrets a number of the choices she made herself. She has several memories she would erase if she possibly could. Some of them she has been able to come to terms with, learn from them and move on. Others still haunt her, clouding every issue in her life and weighing her down with the burden of them. She does the best she can with the life she was dealt, sometimes as an overcomer, other times falling into a victim role. Certainly, when she looks back she thinks of things she would do differently if she could.

How would she define herself? She finds it difficult to see herself as a person in her own right apart from her relationships with other people. In addition, she frets about how she perceives other people define her, affecting how she feels and what she does. Sometimes she puts herself down, even calling herself derogatory names. She tends to judge herself harshly, expecting perfection and intolerant of her mistakes and weaknesses. If she saw the injury she inflicted on her own spirit by doing these things, she would stop doing this. She would never treat her family or friends the same way she treats herself—or would she? Perhaps her self-talk has more of an effect on her relationships than she cares to admit.

Of course, she does possess some qualities that she likes. She tries to make the most of them, developing and strengthening them. She strives to improve herself by imitating the good qualities she sees in others, but it frustrates her when she falls short. More than anything, she wants to be a good person and live up to the potential God placed in her.

Before she had children, she thought she possessed all the knowledge and wisdom she needed to be an expert parent. After giving birth to the first child, she realized she did not have a clue. When other children followed, she was humbled even more. Each child was unique, and what worked for one did not necessarily work for another. Differing personalities meant differing needs. A stern expression might be enough to crush one child, while another required all the disciplinary creativity she could muster. It seemed that every day brought new questions with it, and she had to pray often for wisdom.

She had determined in her youth that she would not do or say some of the things her parents did. Still she often found herself parenting just as they did. Either that or she went to the opposite extreme from them, which was not always best for her children.

She had never dreamed how much the children would be capable of exhausting her, embarrassing her, breaking her heart or testing the limits of her patience. In spite of all that, she loves each one dearly, and there is nothing in the entire world she would trade for them. When they hurt, she hurts; when they are sick, she would gladly take their place; when they pursue an interest, she cheers them on; and when they make bad choices, she loves them anyway.

She is very proud of every milestone they reach and every accomplishment they achieve. As they grow and the older ones begin to leave home and enter into adulthood, she feels that her job is unfinished, but hopes she gave them enough training to live successfully, productively and morally. More than anything, she hopes she did everything she could to connect them to the Lord.

As a young girl, she always wanted to be a wife and mother more than anything else. She dreamed of her handsome prince, and believed he would take care of her and fix all the holes in her wounded heart. She pictured herself happily serving him and finding fulfillment in being the best wife she could be.

She had no way of knowing how unrealistic her expectations were until reality taught her otherwise. Her prince would have wounds of his own, and would seek fulfillment in his own career. He would have expectations of her that she would find challenging to fulfill. Each would have selfishness to overcome, and their ability to forgive severely tested. While they remained true to their commitment to the marriage, they found they did not always like each other very much. There were times when they both wondered if they had made the right choice.

She would never have imagined how challenging it would be for them to communicate on more than a superficial level. She often wondered if they even spoke the same language, because words seemed to mean one thing to her and something entirely different to him. Life brought hardships and trage-dies that sometimes bound them closer together, but sometimes isolated them from each other.

However, they had enough good times and fresh starts to keep them going, together with their deter-mination to honor the vows they made to each other and to God. Each time they persevered through a rough time, better times came and they knew it was worth it to stick together. Besides, they had seen enough homes fall apart and the resulting devasta-tion to convince them to make it work, no matter how much work it took. They could see God's hand in their lives as well, providing what they needed at just the right times. Whether in the form of books, wise counselors, marriage seminars or weekend getaways, opportunities to renew their love or learn better how to live were always available to them.

She found that her career choice as a home-maker was another dream that left her with unful-filled expectations. Daily routines that were fun at the beginning became mundane, and she did not find her responsibilities as rewarding as she thought they would be. Most of the work she did in a day was undone almost as fast as she did it, and she had to do it all over again the next day. When her children were not perfect angels as she had planned for them to be, she felt inadequate as a parent. If they required more attention and the house was in disarray when her husband came home from work, he might ask what she did all day, and the question felt like criticism even if she had a good answer. She knew she was busy all day, but visible results were hard to find.

As much as she struggled, she knew deep in her heart that she had made the right choice, even though the rewards for her labor were sometimes far off in the future. She had seen enough tears in the eyes of other mothers, when they dropped their children off at day care and headed to their jobs, to know what a blessing she had to be able to stay home and nurture her own children. Between observation and conversations with other women, she knew that whether they were homemakers or worked outside the home, they often envied each other and lived with inner conflicts about their roles. Therefore, she continued to fulfill her duties as best she could, reminding herself to be grateful and to wait patiently to see the fruits of her labors. She must trust the Lord that they would come in due time.

She knew she had no friend as faithful and kind as the Lord. Through every trial, disappointment and loss, she sensed His presence and knew she was not alone. She also knew that anything good in her life came from His hand. Sometimes she had a hard time believing He could love someone as unlovable as her, but she chose to trust that He did.

Her early religious training focused on keeping rules out of fear, portraying God as an angry dictator just waiting for her to step out of line so He could condemn her. It took great effort at times to still those voices and believe the message of grace. As she had grown older, she had exposure to more balanced teaching and she studied Him for herself. She came to know Him as a loving Father just waiting for her to turn to Him so He could cleanse, forgive and bless her. As Jesus' sacrificial love became more and more real to her, the motivation to obey Him changed from fear to gratitude. She wanted to please Him because she loved Him. She continues to battle against the tendency to do what she pleases. Her need for grace, and amazement at His willingness to extend it, binds her heart to His and puts a song on her lips and thanksgiving in her heart.

Who is this woman, you ask? She is the person I see gazing back at me every time I look in the mirror. I am learning to accept her, forgive her and even to love her. I have learned that if I am to love my neighbor as myself, I need to have a healthy, honest, humble appreciation of the person God created me to be. I believe He wants me to respect myself and take care of my whole person, body, spirit, mind and soul. Then I will be able to love, serve and give more effectively from a position of wholeness. I still have much to learn and a great deal of growing to do, but I am certain that my Lord walks with me every step of the way.

Who looks back at you from your mirror? When is the last time you moved beyond hair and makeup to study the person you see there, evaluate her needs and appreciate the God-given potential that is hers? Don't you think it's time?

Jesus is standing right there, looking with each of us at the image in the mirror and seeing so much more than we see. He sees a beloved child and loves her enough to die for her. He created her and His work pleases Him. He fashioned her into the unique individual she is, with the blending of personality traits, physical features, gifts, talents, strengths and weaknesses that He saw fit to give her. Then He gave her a free will so that she could choose to love Him or reject Him. Of course, He wants her to love Him, but it must be a choice that she makes or the love is not real.

He gave up the glories of heaven to come and reveal Himself fully, learn to understand what human life on earth is like, and win their love and devotion to Him. He submitted to the rigors of temptation, and so He understands why they so easily fall into the wrong choices, even though He resisted doing so. Because He is not willing to give them up to the evil one, He gave Himself up to bear their punishment in order to be reconciled with them.

Sadly, their free will causes them to inflict tremendous pain on one another at times, and this child in the mirror is no exception. She bears invisible scars on her spirit because of the cruel things that others have said and done to her. Her needs have been ignored or overlooked enough for her to feel invisible herself, and to question her value as a person. Her resulting insecurity drives her at times to look to inadequate sources for worth and fulfillment, and to make choices that are foolish or harmful. He knows, and so does she, that she has treated others badly as well, and she feels the guilt of it. He always stands ready to heal her wounded heart, forgive the sins she foolishly chooses to commit, fill the emptiness she desperately seeks to fill, and teach her to live and love by His example. He knows scars Himself, since in His human body He experienced the cruelty men were capable of inflicting on others. In fact, He kept His scars after His resurrection as another way to relate to His human children (See John 20:27), when He could have risen with a body that was completely made new and free of scars. Therefore, He understands and sympathizes with this lady in the mirror, and He yearns for her to comprehend the depths of His love for her.

If she could hear His audible voice, He would have many things to say to her. He would commend her for recognizing her poverty of spirit, and make the riches of His kingdom available to her. As she mourned over the sin in her life, He would comfort her and encourage her repentance. He would satisfy her hunger and thirst if she sought after righteousness to fill them. He would teach her to show mercy and forgive, just as she had received mercy and forgiveness from Him. He would want her to learn how to please Him, and forget about what anyone else thinks of her. He would want others to see that she is different, treating others the way she wants to be treated, and doing good deeds not to impress people but to give glory to God. If people mistreated her because she belonged to Him, He would bless her richly and reward her greatly in heaven. In fact, He would reward her for everything she did for love of Him in ways that nothing on earth could compare.

He would teach her to value what He values. No earthly treasure could ever measure up to the worth of spending eternity with Him. She needed to stop worrying and focusing so much energy on supplying her physical needs and trust Him to take care of them. She had accumulated so many things that would never last, or could be stolen or blown away by the wind. She would never believe how much of her time was devoted to obtaining, maintaining, retaining and complaining about all the excess "stuff" in her life. She would be richer if she used that time to pursue a deeper relationship with Him and to care for the people He brought into her life. She could either give away or sell many of her possessions without ever missing them. By doing so, she could help others who needed things she had and could not afford to buy them. Her life would be simpler then, and she could count herself wealthy in relationships by investing more time and effort in them.

He would remind her of the many ways the Father showed His love throughout her life. She could ask Him for anything, and He would give it to her if He determined it to be for her good. In fact, she could look back on some of the times when He denied her requests, and thank Him for it because she saw that He knew what was best for her. Additionally, He would reveal Himself to her if she sought Him, and open His door to her if she knocked on it. He loved to give good gifts to His children more than the very best of earthly fathers did (See Matthew 5-7). He tended to her better than the very best of shepherds tended his sheep (John 10:1-15). He fed her the bread of life and satisfied her thirst with living water (John 6:35). He gave the supreme gift of His Son to release her from condemnation and save her from perishing (John 3:16-17). She could walk in His light and find continual cleansing in the blood poured out for her (1 John 1:7). He gave her life purpose and meaning, and empowered her to live abundantly, in faith rather than in fear.

Once she learned to find security in His love for her, He would teach her to imitate Him in her way of life. He would direct her focus away from trying to do religious things right and toward doing relational things right. He desired that she obey Him out of deep love and gratitude for Him rather than fear of punishment. He wanted her to spend time in prayer and His word for companionship with Him, not out of obligation. He would train her to love as He loved, serve as He served and give as He gave. In the same way that He noticed people others overlooked, touched people others avoided, loved people others despised, and ministered to people others ignored, He would instruct her to do the same.

The more she did these things, the greater her joy and the more satisfying her life would be. He would give her rest for her weariness, healing for her brokenness, fulfillment for her emptiness, mercy for her sinfulness and love for her loneliness. When she grasped all that He offered her, she would return to Him glory, honor, praise, worship, thanksgiving, adoration and devotion. After all, she would then be fulfilling the very purpose for which He created her.

Take a closer look:
1. Read the following verses about self, and formulate a description of a healthy view of yourself:
   Matthew 16:24; 18:4; 22:39; 23:12
   Mark 12:33
   Luke 6:42; 9:25; 12:20-21; 18:11-14
   John 15:4
   Romans 2:1, 7-8 & 21; 6:6; 12:3; 13:1;
     14:7,12,22; 15:3
   1 Corinthians 2:15-16; 6:15-20; 9:19,27;
     11:28-29; 13:5
   2 Corinthians 10:18
   Galatians 6:1-5
   Ephesians 4:22-24
   Philippians 2:3-8
   Colossians 3:9-10
   1 Thessalonians 5:6-8
   1 Timothy 4:7, 13-16; 5:22
   2 Timothy 1:7; 2:15, 21
   Titus 2:2-6, 12
   James 1:22-27; 3:14-16; 5:5
   1 Peter 1:13; 3:3-4; 4:7; 5:8
   2 Peter 1:5-9
   1 John 3:1-4
2. Look through the gospels (with a red-letter edition of the Bible if you have one), read Jesus' words, and consider the following:
   a. How did He describe Himself?

b. How did He describe the Father, and what did He say about Him?

c. When He gave a rebuke, what offended Him? What angered Him?

d. What pleased Him? What are His requirements for righteous living?

Conclusion

How is your eyesight? Has your vision changed? Is your focus clearer? My prayer is that reading this book and studying the Scriptures has helped you to see Jesus and the people who interacted with Him in a completely new way. They were real, live human beings with feelings, dreams, and needs like you and me. Jesus showed us how He values each person, looks beyond his or her exterior, and meets every need with love and compassion.

I hope your way of looking at the people around you will never be the same. There are people who cross your path every day that you have never noticed before. I am optimistic that you will notice them from now on. People you live with, work with, and see every day may have become commonplace to you. I trust that you will observe them with fresh eyes. Someone near you feels left out, lonely and unwanted. I pray you will befriend them. People in need are all around you. They may be sick, poor, sinful, troubled or weary. I hope you will reach out to them with the love of Jesus.

Have you made friends with the woman in your mirror? She needs you to be kind to her and take care of her. It is important that you see her as she is, but allow Jesus to help her become all that He created her to be. Appreciate His design and admire His creativity in her construction. Then forget about her as you focus your attention on knowing, worshipping, serving and loving Him every day of your life. A more beautiful sight than His lovely face your eyes will never behold. Your eyesight will never be the same!

Printed in the United States
72982LV00001B/1-240